Cooking
with
Mary Berry

Cooking
with
Mary Berry

DK | Penguin Random House

First American Edition, 2016
Published in the United States
by DK Publishing
345 Hudson Street
New York, New York 10014

A catalog record for this book is available
from the Library of Congress.
ISBN 978-1-4654-5951-0

DK books are available at special discounts
when purchased in bulk for sales
promotions, premiums, fund-raising, or
educational use. For details, contact:
DK Publishing Special Markets
345 Hudson Street
New York, New York 10014
SpecialSales@dk.com

Printed and bound in China

All images © Dorling Kindersley Limited
For further information see:
www.dkimages.com

A WORLD OF IDEAS:
SEE ALL THERE IS TO KNOW

www.dk.com

Contents

INTRODUCTION

People often ask how I decide which recipes to feature in a book. Here, I have included the sort of recipes that, when I've made them for my family, they exclaim, "Ooh, that's good, mum. It's the best I've ever had!" I always tell myself that my recipes have to check three boxes: look good, taste good, and be practical to make. That is my aim.

You should find the recipes here fairly easy. When I develop recipes, I try to keep them simple. I use a limited number of ingredients per recipe, and avoid complicated ones. I don't want to send you out searching for a specialty spice that will then gather dust in your pantry and never be used again. The ingredients I use can be found without difficulty, and they are ones that you are likely to choose time and time again.

I always break up the method into stages and then number the stages. This is so helpful. If you are interrupted halfway through cooking—perhaps the front doorbell rings—it's easy to remember where you have reached in the recipe. And if there are any slightly tricky stages, we demonstrate them with a step-by-step.

All the recipes that go in my cookbooks are well tried and tested. In my kitchen at home (which is a cozy family kitchen), my small team and I test and taste, and test and taste, and test and taste until we have an easy method that gives wonderful results.

I'm not averse to a little cheating. If a recipe calls for dough and I can buy good quality dough, I will. One thing I do not cheat on, though, is herbs. I always use fresh herbs now. They taste completely different than dried herbs, which are more sharp and piquant.

Something I love about judging the *Great Holiday Baking Show* is that the "guests" often bake specialties from their own regions. In this book, among the everyday favorites, you will find some recipes that may be less familiar. These are the specialties of my own region, England. The Bath buns are from the city where I grew up. Do try them!

Bath buns

Mary Berry

TECHNIQUES

Egg know-how

Eggs are one of the most useful tools in a cook's repertoire. They can be cooked in many delicious ways, from simple boiling and poaching to omelets and soufflés. Whichever type of egg you buy (hen's, duck's, quail's), choose the ones with the longest "use-by" date, and make sure none are cracked.

Separating eggs

For best results, take eggs straight from the fridge so they are well chilled.

1 Holding an egg over a bowl, break open the shell. Carefully transfer the yolk from one half shell to the other, letting the egg white run into the bowl. Repeat several times.

2 Put the yolk in another bowl. Remove any yolk from the white with the tip of a spoon (the white will not whisk if there is any trace of yolk).

Cooking eggs

Frying
Fresh eggs are essential for successful frying because they keep their shape during cooking. Fry the eggs in your favorite oil, adding a pat of butter for extra flavor if you like.

1 Heat a thin layer of oil in a nonstick frying pan. When the oil is very hot and starting to sizzle, slip in an egg and cook over medium heat.

2 Spoon the oil over once or twice to give a white top. Remove and serve, or turn over and cook for a few seconds, to set the yolk a little more.

Scrambling
Scrambled eggs can be served plain, or flavored with herbs, cheese, ham, or smoked salmon. Allow 2 eggs per person.

1 Lightly beat the eggs with salt and pepper to taste and a little milk, if you like. Melt a pat of butter in a pan. Add the eggs.

2 Cook over medium heat, stirring constantly with a wooden spatula or spoon, until almost set—they will continue to cook after they have been removed from the heat. Serve at once.

Poaching

The classic method for poaching eggs is in a pan of simmering water. Use the freshest eggs possible, as they will keep a neat shape.

1 Bring a wide pan of water to a boil. Lower the heat so that the water is simmering, and slide in an egg. Swirl the water around the egg to give it a neat shape. Simmer for 3–4 minutes until the egg is cooked to your taste.

2 Lift out the egg with a slotted spoon and drain briefly on paper towels. To keep them warm, or to reheat them if they have been prepared ahead, immerse them in a bowl of hot water (they will take 1 minute to reheat).

Making crêpes

The quantities given here will make enough batter for about 12 thin crêpes, using a 7–8in (18–20cm) pan. Do not worry if the first crêpe or two is a failure: it acts as a test for the consistency of the batter and the heat of the pan.

1 Sift 1 cup all-purpose flour into a bowl and make a well in the middle. Whisk together 1 large egg, 1 large egg yolk, and a little milk taken from 1¼ cups, then pour into the well. Whisk with a little of the flour.

2 Gradually whisk in half of the remaining milk, drawing in the rest of the flour a little at a time, to make a smooth batter. Stir in the remaining milk. Cover and let stand for about 30 minutes.

3 Heat the frying pan and brush with a little oil. Ladle 2–3 tablespoons of batter into the pan and tilt the pan so that the batter spreads out evenly over the bottom.

4 Cook the crêpe over medium–high heat for 45–60 seconds until small holes appear on the surface, the underside is lightly browned, and the edges have started to curl. Loosen the crêpe and turn it over by tossing or flipping it with a spatula. Cook the other side for about 30 seconds until golden.

5 Slide the crêpe out of the pan. Heat and lightly grease the pan again before making the next crêpe. Serve the crêpes as they are made, or stack them on a plate and reheat before serving. (If the crêpes are hot when you stack them, they will not stick together; there is no need to interleave them with wax paper.)

Cooking meat

For centuries, meat has been the protein food around which the majority of meals have been planned. But today, healthy eating advice suggests making meat and other protein foods just one part of a healthy diet, not the major part. By making sure the cooking method suits the cut of meat you are preparing—quick cooking for lean meats, long, slow cooking for tougher cuts—you will always have perfectly moist and tender results.

Basic cooking techniques

Tougher pieces of meat should be cooked slowly by stewing or braising to make them beautifully tender. Those cuts that are naturally tender can be cooked quickly by frying.

Braising

1 Brown the meat on all sides in a Dutch oven to add flavor and a rich color. Remove the meat from the pot.

2 Add vegetables and cook until beginning to brown. Return the meat and add liquid and any flavorings. Bring to a boil, then cover and cook gently on the stove or in the oven, as instructed in the recipe.

Stewing

Cut the meat into cubes. Put into a Dutch oven with any vegetables and liquid to cover plus any flavorings. Bring to a boil, then cover and simmer on the stove or cook in the oven. Alternatively, heat some oil in the pot and brown the cubes of meat, then brown the vegetables. Add the liquid and any flavorings. Bring to a boil, cover, and simmer.

Roasting

1 Remove the meat from the refrigerator and let it come to room temperature.

2 Preheat the oven. Rub the meat with fat or oil and seasonings, or make incisions all over and insert herbs or slivers of garlic. Insert a meat thermometer, if using.

3 Put the meat and any vegetables in a roasting pan. Roast, basting with the fat and juices in the pan, until cooked to your taste. If not using a meat thermometer, test whether the meat is cooked by inserting a skewer into the center. If the juices that run out are bloody, the meat is rare; if pink, medium; if clear, well-done.

4 Transfer the meat to a carving board and let rest for 10–15 minutes. Carve and serve.

Cooking poultry thoroughly

Cook poultry thoroughly to kill any bacteria.

To test a whole roasted bird, lift it on a long fork—the juices that run out should be clear. For pieces, insert a skewer into the thickest part of the meat and check the color of the juices. Alternatively, use an instant-read thermometer: the thigh meat should register 170°F (75°C), breast 160°F (70°C).

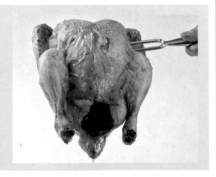

Broiling and barbecuing

1 Preheat the broiler to hot, or light the grill (it will take 20–30 minutes to reach cooking temperature unless it is gas, which will heat up immediately).

2 Put the meat on a broiling pan and put under the hot broiler, or arrange on the rack over charcoal. Brush with oil or a marinade and cook the meat until it is browned, turning and rebrushing.

3 For sausages or thicker pieces of meat that need to be well cooked, reduce the heat or move the meat farther away from the heat and complete cooking.

Stir-frying

1 Cut the meat into uniform pieces for even cooking. Heat a wok or heavy frying pan, then add a little oil. When the oil is hot, start adding the meat, a little at a time—adding too much at once will lower the temperature of the oil. Using a slotted spoon or a spatula, stir and toss the meat constantly until it is evenly browned.

2 If some of the pieces of meat are cooked before others, they can be pushed up the side of the wok or to the side of the pan where they will keep warm but not overcook.

Frying and sautéing

1 Dry the meat with paper towels (if too moist it will not brown quickly and evenly). Heat oil or a mixture of oil and butter in a heavy frying pan until it is very hot, then add the meat, being careful not to crowd the pan.

2 Cook until well browned on both sides. Reduce the heat and continue cooking until the meat is done to your taste. When turning meat, use tongs rather than a fork, as a fork pierces the meat and allows the juices to run out.

Meat stock

Ask your butcher to saw 4lb (2kg) bones into 2½in (6cm) pieces. Beef and veal bones are best.

1 Roast the bones in a preheated oven at 450°F (230°C) for 30 minutes. Add 2–3 coarsely chopped onions, carrots, and celery stalks and roast for 30 minutes.

2 Transfer to a large stockpot. Add 4 quarts (4 liters) water, a bouquet garni made of 1–2 bay leaves, a few parsley stalks, 1–2 sprigs of thyme, and a few black peppercorns.

3 Bring to a boil. Skim off foam, then cover and simmer for 4–6 hours. Ladle into a sieve to strain. Skim off fat, or let cool and lift off solidified fat.

Fish and shellfish know-how

Seafood is delicious, versatile, and quick to cook. It is also very nutritious: all fish and shellfish are good sources of essential vitamins and minerals, but oily fish is particularly rich in vitamins A and D and also provides beneficial omega-3 fatty acids.

Cleaning and boning whole fish

Whole fish such as trout, snapper, herring, and salmon are delicious, and boning makes them easier to serve and eat. When boned they can also be stuffed. Seafood markets will prepare the fish for you, but if you want to do it yourself, here's how.

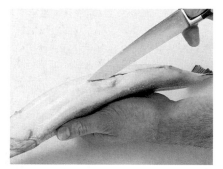

1 To clean the fish, first snip off the fins. Cut along the belly, from the vent end to just below the head. Remove the innards, scraping away any dark blood. Lift the gill covering and remove the accordion-shaped gills. Rinse well.

2 To bone, extend the belly opening so that it goes all the way to the tail. Hold the belly open and carefully run the knife between the flesh and the bones along one side, from tail to head, to cut the flesh from the rib cage.

3 Turn the fish around and cut the flesh from the rib cage on the other side. Snip through the backbone at each end and gently pull it away from the flesh, removing it with the rib cage in one piece.

4 If the head and tail have been cut off, open out the fish and lay it skin-side up. Press along the backbone to loosen the bones. Turn over and lift or cut out the rib cage and backbone. The fish is now "butterflied."

Buying and storing

When buying fish and shellfish, aroma and appearance are your guides. Seafood should have the clean smell of the sea. If it has an unpleasantly "fishy" or ammonia-like odor, it is not fresh.

Whole fresh fish should have clean, red gills, the scales should be firmly attached, and it should be covered in a clear slime; the flesh should feel firm and springy. The flesh of fillets and steaks should be firm, moist, and lustrous. If buying prepackaged fish, check the color of any liquid in the package: it should not be cloudy or off-white.

Shellfish is sold both in the shell and shelled, raw and cooked. The shells of crabs, lobsters, and shrimp become pink or red when cooked. Live shellfish, such as mussels, clams, and oysters, should have tightly closed shells. If any shells are open, they should close if lightly tapped; if they do not, the shellfish is dead and should be discarded. Shelled oysters, scallops, and clams should be plump; scallops should smell slightly sweet. Shrimp should also smell faintly sweet, and feel firm.

Keep cool until you get home, then unwrap it, cover with a wet cloth or wet paper towels, and store in the coldest part of the refrigerator. Use oily fish and shellfish the same day; keep white fish no more than 24 hours.

Freezing

It's best to buy fish that is flash-frozen, as it will have been processed and frozen at very low temperatures immediately after being caught—while still at sea—to prevent any deterioration.

If you have fish to freeze yourself, clean it and wrap tightly. For the best flavor, store white fish for no longer than 3 months, oily fish and shellfish for 2 months. (When buying, be aware that some seafood sold as "fresh" may have been frozen and then thawed, so it should not be frozen again at home.)

Fish fillets and some shellfish can be cooked very successfully from frozen, but if you need to thaw seafood before cooking, do so slowly in the refrigerator or quickly in the microwave. When using a microwave, arrange pieces of fish so that the thicker areas are at the outside of the dish; overlap thin areas or fold them under.

Scaling

Unless you are skinning a fish before cooking, the scales should be removed. Dip your fingers in salt to ensure a firm grip and grasp the fish tail. Using the blunt side of a knife, with firm strokes scrape off the scales, from tail to head. Rinse well. Or ask your seafood market to do this.

Fish stock

Ask your market for heads, bones, and trimmings from lean white fish (not oily fish, which make a bitter-tasting stock).

Rinse 1½lb (675) bones and trimmings and put them into a large pan. Add 4 cups water and 1 cup dry white wine. Bring to a boil, skimming the surface.

Add 1 sliced onion, 1 sliced carrot, 1 chopped celery stalk, 1 bay leaf, a few parsley sprigs, and a few black peppercorns. Simmer for 20–25 minutes. Strain. Use immediately, or cool, cover, and refrigerate to use within 2 days. It can also be frozen for up to 3 months.

Filleting flat fish

Either 2 wide or 4 narrow fillets can be cut from a small flat fish. Larger flat fish will yield 4 good-sized fillets. Keep the bones for making stock.

1 Make a shallow cut through the skin around the edge of the fish, where the fin bones meet the body. Cut across the tail and make a curved cut around the head. Then cut down the center of the fish, cutting through the flesh to the bone.

2 Insert the knife between the flesh and the bones on one side at the head end. Keeping the knife almost parallel to the fish, cut close to the bones, loosening the flesh to detach the fillet in one piece.

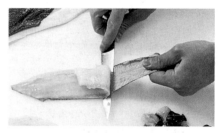

3 Repeat to remove the second fillet on the same side, then turn the fish over and remove both of the fillets from the other side. Check the fillets for any stray bones, pulling them out with tweezers.

4 To skin, lay each fillet skin-side down and hold the tail with salted fingers to ensure a firm grip. Cut through the flesh at the tail end; then, holding the knife at an angle, cut the flesh from the skin.

Preparing mussels and clams

Most mussels and clams are sold live and are cooked by steaming in their shells. They must be scrubbed before cooking. The anchoring threads found on mussels, known as beards, must also be removed.

To clean the shells of mussels and clams, hold under cold running water and scrub with a small stiff brush. Use a small knife to scrape off any barnacles. To remove the beard from a mussel, hold the beard firmly between your thumb and the blade of a small knife and pull the beard away from the shell.

Vegetable know-how

On every shopping trip there seems to be more new vegetables to try—strangely shaped squashes, tomatoes and bell peppers of all colors, exotic mushrooms, and salad greens. This wonderful variety enables a cook to be innovative, creating nutritious, appetizing dishes with minimum effort.

Cooking vegetables

Choose the right cooking method to bring out the best in vegetables and create exciting accompaniments or main dishes. If cooking a variety of vegetables at the same time, remember some take longer to cook than others, so you may have to add them in stages.

Baking
Potatoes, sweet potatoes, eggplant, and pumpkin are all delicious baked. Prick the skins of whole vegetables or, if cut, moisten cut surfaces with oil or butter. Push a skewer through the centers of large vegetables to conduct heat and speed up cooking time.

Boiling
Drop vegetables into a large pan of boiling salted water and bring back to a boil as quickly as possible. Simmer until just tender, then drain. To stop further cooking and set the color of green vegetables, rinse briefly under cold running water.

Steaming
Bring water to a boil in a steamer base. Put the vegetables in a single layer on the rack, cover, and steam until just tender. If you don't have a steamer, use a large saucepan with a steamer basket, or a wok and a bamboo steamer.

Deep-frying
Heat oil in a deep fryer to the required temperature. Add the vegetables in batches and fry until golden, bringing the oil back to the required temperature between each batch. Drain on paper towels.

Roasting
Cut vegetables into chunks and blanch. Drain. Put olive oil or duck fat into a roasting pan and heat in a preheated 350°F (180°C) oven. Add vegetables and turn to coat with the fat. Roast, turning occasionally, until browned.

Sautéing
Cook the vegetables in oil over high heat, stirring and turning constantly, until they start to brown. Reduce the heat and continue cooking, stirring occasionally, until tender.

Braising

Carrots, celery, and other root vegetables are ideal for braising. Put the vegetables into a heavy pan or Dutch oven, add a small amount of water or stock, and bring to a boil. Cover tightly and cook over low heat until just tender. Boil to evaporate the liquid or drain.

Stir-frying

Cut the vegetables into small, even-sized pieces. Heat a little oil in a wok. When it is hot, add the vegetables, starting with those that need the longest cooking time. Keep the heat high, and toss and stir the vegetables constantly. Cook for just a few minutes until tender but still crisp.

Grilling

Many types of quick-cooking vegetables can be cooked on an outdoor grill as well as under a broiler. Halve the vegetables or cut into thick slices. Brush with oil and grill, turning at least once, until tender. For extra flavor, marinate the vegetables first (page 192).

Freezing

Most vegetables freeze very well, whether plain, in a sauce, or in a prepared dish. The exceptions are potatoes and watery vegetables like cucumbers and tomatoes. Vegetables that are to be frozen plain should be very fresh. Before freezing, blanch them in boiling water, then cool quickly in iced water; this will set the fresh color. Vegetables can be kept in the freezer for 6–12 months, and can be cooked directly from frozen.

Cutting vegetables

Keep pieces to a uniform size and shape to ensure they cook evenly.

Julienne

Cut into ¼in (5mm) slices. Stack the slices, then cut into sticks ¼in (5mm) thick.

Dice

Cut into ½in (1cm) strips, then cut across the strips to form neat cubes.

Ribbons

Using a vegetable peeler, carefully shave off thin, wide ribbons.

Making desserts

Chilled desserts can be made well in advance so they are great for dinner parties. Fruit salads, trifles, creamy mousses and light chilled soufflés, meringue baskets, gâteaux, rich cheesecakes, layered terrines, ice creams, and sorbets—all can be kept in the refrigerator or freezer, to be served when you're ready.

Whisking egg whites

A balloon whisk is the classic tool for whisking egg whites, but an electric mixer saves time and effort. Ensure all your equipment is clean, dry, and grease-free, and that the egg whites are at room temperature.

Whisk the whites as forcefully as possible (on maximum speed if using an electric mixer) right from the start. When they look like a cloud, add any sugar little by little. The mixture will get stiffer and stiffer as you add sugar and whisk.

Folding egg whites

To retain as much air as possible, egg whites should be folded gently and quickly into a mixture.

Mix a spoonful of the whites into the heavy mixture to lighten it. Using a rubber spatula or metal spoon, fold in the remaining whites using a figure-eight motion, cutting straight through the mixture, then turning it over until well blended.

Preparing citrus fruits

When taking the zest from citrus fruits, first scrub the fruit with hot soapy water, rinse well, and dry.

Segmenting

Hold the peeled fruit over a bowl to catch the juice. With a sharp knife, cut down one side of a segment, cutting it from the dividing membrane. Cut away from the membrane on the other side and remove the segment. Continue all around the fruit.

Dissolving gelatin

Gelatin is a flavorless setting agent used in chilled desserts such as fruit jellies. It is most commonly available as a powder, in packages. Gelatin sheets can also be used (4 sheets in place of 1 package): soften in cold water for 5 minutes, then drain and melt in the hot dessert mixture, whisking well.

1 Put the given quantity of cold water or other liquid into a small heatproof bowl and sprinkle the given quantity of gelatin over the surface. Let soak for about 10 minutes until the gelatin has absorbed the liquid and become spongy.

2 Put the bowl of gelatin into a pan of hot water and heat until the gelatin has dissolved and is clear. Use a metal spoon to check that there are no granules left. Use the gelatin at the same temperature as the mixture it is setting.

Decorating with chocolate

Chocolate decorations can transform a dessert, and you don't have to reserve them for desserts made only from chocolate—fruit salads and mousses can also benefit from a contrasting finishing touch.

Chocolate curls

Have the chocolate at room temperature, and use a peeler to shave off long curls onto a sheet of parchment paper. Lift the paper to transfer the curls onto the dessert.

Chocolate shavings

1 Spread a smooth, thin layer of melted chocolate, about ⅟₁₆in (1.5mm) thick, onto a cool work surface (preferably marble), and let cool until nearly set.

2 Using a long, sharp knife held at an angle, push across the chocolate with a slight sawing action to shave it into shaved curls.

Decorating with cream

Piped whipped cream adds a professional touch to desserts and cakes, and with a little practice and some confidence this is not difficult to do. A star-shaped nozzle or decorating tip is the most useful.

1 Drop the nozzle into the piping bag, then tuck the lower half of the piping bag into the nozzle to prevent the cream from leaking out when filling the bag.

2 Hold the bag in one hand, folding the top of the bag over your hand. Spoon in the whipped cream.

3 When the bag is full, twist the top until there is no air left. Pipe the cream as desired, gently squeezing the twisted end to force out the cream in a steady stream.

Rosette

Hold the bag upright, just above the surface of the cake. Squeeze gently, moving the bag in a small circle. Stop squeezing and lift the nozzle away.

Swirl

Hold the bag upright, just above the surface of the cake. Squeeze the bag and pipe the cream in a steady stream, guiding the nozzle in an "S" shape.

Rope

Hold the bag at a 45° angle. Pipe a short length of cream to one side. Pipe another length of cream to the opposite side, overlapping the first one.

BREAKFASTS AND BRUNCHES

MUSHROOM OMELET
with ciabatta

SERVES 2   673 CALS PER SERVING

Ingredients

4 large eggs

salt and black pepper

2 tbsp butter

2oz (60g) shiitake
  mushrooms, sliced

1 tbsp snipped fresh chives

1 loaf of ciabatta bread,
  warmed and split
  lengthwise

1 Break the eggs into a small bowl, season with salt and pepper, and beat with a fork.

2 Melt half of the butter in a small frying pan, add the mushrooms, and cook over high heat for 3–5 minutes until all the liquid has evaporated. Remove from the heat, stir in the chives, season with salt and pepper, and keep hot.

3 Heat an omelet pan or small frying pan until very hot. Add the remaining butter and swirl the pan to evenly coat the base and sides. When the butter is foaming, pour in the seasoned egg mixture.

4 Cook the omelet over medium heat, pulling back the edge as the eggs set, and tilting the pan to allow the uncooked egg to run to the side of the pan. Continue until the omelet is lightly set and the underside is golden brown. Remove from the heat.

5 Scatter the mushrooms over half of the omelet, then flip the uncovered half over them. Fill the warmed split ciabatta with the omelet, cut the ciabatta in half crosswise, and serve at once.

MEXICAN
omelet

MAKES 2   547 CALS EACH

Ingredients

Filling

2 tbsp olive oil

1 onion, finely chopped

1 garlic clove, crushed

1 green bell pepper, halved, seeded, and finely chopped

2 ripe tomatoes, finely chopped

4oz (125g) button mushrooms, thinly sliced

¼ tsp Worcestershire sauce

a few drops of hot pepper sauce

salt and black pepper

For the omelet

6 large eggs

2 tbsp butter

chopped parsley to garnish

VARIATION

SMOKED CHICKEN
omelet

Substitute 4oz (125g) diced smoked chicken and 1 tbsp snipped fresh chives for the filling.

1 Make the filling: heat the oil in a frying pan, add the onion and garlic, and cook for 5 minutes or until softened. Add the bell pepper and cook, stirring, for 5 minutes.

2 Add the tomatoes and mushrooms and cook, stirring, for 10 minutes. Add the Worcestershire and hot pepper sauces, season with salt and pepper, and simmer for about 5 minutes. Keep warm.

3 Beat 3 of the eggs in a bowl with salt and pepper. Heat an omelet pan or small frying pan and add half of the butter.

4 When the butter is foaming, add the eggs and cook over medium heat, pulling back the edge as the eggs set, and tilting the pan so the liquid egg runs underneath. Continue until lightly set and golden.

5 Spoon half of the filling onto the half of the omelet farthest from the pan handle. With an offset spatula, lift the uncovered half of the omelet and flip it over the filling.

6 Slide the omelet onto a warmed plate and garnish with chopped parsley. Make the second omelet in the same way, reheating the pan before adding the butter.

ZUCCHINI
and prosciutto frittata

SERVES 4   270 CALS PER SERVING

Ingredients

2 tbsp olive oil

1¼lb (625g) small zucchini, thinly sliced on a diagonal

6 large eggs

salt and black pepper

2oz (60g) prosciutto, diced

shredded fresh basil or chopped flat-leaf parsley to garnish

1 Heat the olive oil in a large frying pan. Add the zucchini and cook gently for 5 minutes or until just tender.

2 Break the eggs into a bowl, season with salt and pepper, and beat with a fork.

3 Add the prosciutto to the zucchini in the frying pan, then pour in the eggs.

4 Cook over medium heat for about 10 minutes. As the eggs set, lift the frittata with a spatula and tilt the pan to allow the uncooked egg to run underneath. Continue until almost set and the underside is golden brown.

5 Place the frying pan under a hot broiler, 4in (10cm) from the heat, for 1–2 minutes until the top is a light golden brown color and the egg is cooked through and quite firm when pressed.

6 Cut the frittata into wedges and lightly garnish with shredded fresh basil or chopped parsley. Serve hot or cold.

CHICKEN CRÊPES
florentine

MAKES 8   360 CALS EACH

Ingredients

Filling

4 tbsp butter

12oz (350g) cremini
  mushrooms, quartered

⅓ cup all-purpose flour

1¼ cups chicken stock

12oz (350g) boneless and
  skinless cooked chicken,
  cut into bite-sized pieces

1 tbsp chopped
  fresh tarragon

salt and black pepper

For the crêpes

1lb (500g) spinach leaves,
  coarsely chopped

2 tbsp butter

pinch of grated nutmeg

8 crêpes (page 11)

4oz (125g) Gruyère
  cheese, grated

1 Preheat the oven to 375°F (190°C). Make the filling: melt the butter in a heavy pan, add the mushrooms, and cook, stirring often, for 2–3 minutes.

2 Add the flour and cook, stirring, for 1 minute. Remove the pan from the heat and gradually blend in the stock. Bring to a boil, stirring, and simmer for 2–3 minutes. Add the chicken and tarragon and season with salt and pepper.

3 Rinse the spinach and put into a saucepan with only the water that clings to the leaves. Cook for 2 minutes or until tender. Drain well, squeezing to extract any excess water, then stir in the butter and nutmeg. Spoon into a shallow ovenproof dish.

4 Divide the chicken and mushroom mixture among the 8 crêpes. Roll up the crêpes and place them in a single layer on top of the spinach.

5 Sprinkle with the cheese and bake for about 25 minutes until golden. Serve hot.

KEDGEREE

SERVES 4   470 CALS PER SERVING

Ingredients

1 cup long-grain rice

¼ tsp turmeric

12oz (350g) smoked
  haddock fillet

2 hard-boiled eggs, peeled

4 tbsp butter, plus
  extra for greasing

juice of ½ lemon

⅔ cup half-and-half

salt

cayenne pepper

2 tbsp finely
  chopped parsley

1 Preheat the oven to 350°F (180°C). Simmer the rice and turmeric, covered, in boiling salted water for 12–15 minutes until tender. Rinse with hot water, drain, and keep warm.

2 Meanwhile, put the haddock, skin-side down, in a frying pan, cover with cold water, and poach for 8–10 minutes.

3 Cut 1 egg lengthwise into quarters and reserve for garnish. Coarsely chop the second egg.

4 Drain the haddock, remove the skin and bones, then flake the fish. Put the fish into a large bowl; add the rice, chopped egg, butter, lemon juice, and half-and-half; and season with salt and cayenne pepper. Stir gently to mix.

5 Butter an ovenproof dish, add the kedgeree, and bake, stirring occasionally, for 10–15 minutes.

6 To serve, stir in the parsley and garnish with the reserved egg quarters.

Kedgeree

This delicately spiced rice dish has been a British breakfast favorite for centuries and makes for a perfect weekend treat.

STRATA
with cheese and pesto

SERVES 4   600 CALS PER SERVING

Ingredients

4–6 thick slices of
 stale bread

¼– ⅓ cup store-bought
 pesto

4 large eggs, lightly beaten

½ cup crème fraîche

½ cup milk

6oz (175g) Fontina or aged
 Cheddar cheese, grated

2oz (60g) mozzarella
 cheese, grated

1oz (30g) Parmesan
 cheese, grated

1 Preheat the oven to 400°F (200°C). Cut off and discard the crusts from the bread. Spread the slices with pesto, then arrange them in a single layer in a baking dish.

2 In a bowl, combine the eggs with the crème fraîche and milk, then pour over the bread. Sprinkle with the grated cheeses.

3 Bake the strata for 35–40 minutes until golden brown. It will puff up slightly as it bakes but, unlike a soufflé, it can be safely left to stand for about 5 minutes before serving. A simple tomato salad makes a perfect accompaniment.

Cook's know-how

You need stale bread to make a good, moist strata (a Californian recipe for using up leftover bread). If the bread is fresh, the strata will be soggy.

Strata

A classic brunch dish. Add slices of vegetables or ham for a more filling meal.

CROQUE SEÑOR

SERVES 4   413 CALS PER SERVING

Ingredients

Spicy tomato salsa

3 ripe but firm tomatoes, finely chopped

1 red bell pepper, halved, seeded, roasted, and peeled (see box, below), finely chopped

1 garlic clove, crushed

2 scallions, thinly sliced

1 fresh green jalapeño, halved, seeded, and chopped

1 tbsp red wine vinegar

salt

For the sandwich

8 slices of white bread

4 slices of aged Cheddar cheese

4 slices of ham

2 tbsp butter, softened

lemon wedges and cilantro sprigs to serve

1 Make the salsa: combine the tomatoes, red bell pepper, garlic, scallions, jalapeño, and vinegar in a bowl. Season with salt and set aside.

2 Put 4 slices of bread onto a board and arrange the cheese slices, then the ham slices, on top. Spoon the salsa over the ham.

3 Lightly spread the butter over one side of the remaining slices of bread and put them, butter-side up, on top of the salsa.

4 Heat a heavy frying pan and cook each sandwich, butter-side down, over medium-high heat until the cheese begins to melt and the bread becomes golden. Lightly spread the second side of each sandwich with butter. Turn over and cook the other side until golden.

5 Garnish with lemon wedges, cilantro sprigs, and any remaining spicy tomato salsa. Serve hot.

ROASTING AND PEELING BELL PEPPERS

Cook the bell pepper halves, cut-side down, under a hot broiler, 4in (10cm) from the heat, until the skin is black and blistered. Seal in a plastic bag and let cool. Peel off the skin, using your fingers.

EGGS BENEDICT

SERVES 4   602 CALS PER SERVING

Ingredients

8 slices thick-cut Canadian
 bacon

2 English muffins, halved

4 large eggs

butter for spreading

fresh flat-leaf parsley
 to garnish

Hollandaise sauce

2 tsp lemon juice

2 tsp white wine vinegar

3 large egg yolks, at
 room temperature

8 tbsp unsalted
 butter, melted

salt and black pepper

1 Cook the bacon under a hot broiler, 3in (7cm) from the heat, for 5–7 minutes until crisp. Keep the bacon warm.

2 Toast the cut sides of the English muffin halves under the broiler. Keep warm.

3 Make the hollandaise sauce: put the lemon juice and wine vinegar into a small bowl, add the egg yolks, and whisk with a balloon whisk until light and frothy.

4 Place the bowl over a pan of simmering water and whisk until the mixture thickens. Gradually add the melted butter, whisking constantly until thick. Season. Keep warm.

5 Poach the eggs: bring a large pan of water to a boil. Lower the heat so that the water is simmering, and slide in the eggs. Swirl the water around the eggs to make neat shapes. Simmer for about 4 minutes. Lift out with a slotted spoon.

6 Butter the English muffin halves and put onto warmed plates. Put 2 slices of bacon and an egg on each one and top with the sauce. Serve at once, garnished with parsley.

VARIATION

SPICY LIME
hollandaise

Substitute 2 tsp lime juice for the lemon juice in the hollandaise sauce, and add $1/2$ tsp each of paprika and mild chili powder.

SOUPS, SALADS, AND APPETIZERS

FRENCH ONION soup

SERVES 8   353 CALS PER SERVING

Ingredients

3 tbsp butter

1 tbsp sunflower oil

2lb (1kg) large white onions, thinly sliced

2 tsp granulated sugar

¼ cup all-purpose flour

7½ cups vegetable, chicken, or beef stock

salt and black pepper

8 Gruyère croûtes (see below)

1 Melt the butter with the oil in a large saucepan and caramelize the onions with the sugar (see box, below). Sprinkle the flour into the pan and cook, stirring constantly, for 1–2 minutes.

2 Gradually stir in the stock and bring to a boil. Season with salt and pepper, then cover and simmer, stirring from time to time, for 35 minutes.

3 Taste the soup for seasoning, then ladle into warmed bowls. Float a Gruyère croûte in each bowl and serve at once.

Gruyère croûtes

Cut slices from a baguette and toast on one side under a hot grill. Remove from the heat and turn over. Grate Gruyère cheese evenly over the untoasted sides of the bread slices. Return to the grill and cook until the cheese has melted and is gently bubbling.

CARAMELIZING ONIONS

Cook the onions in the butter and oil for a few minutes until soft. Add the sugar and continue cooking over low heat, stirring occasionally, for 20 minutes or until the onions are golden brown.

VEGETABLE
minestrone

SERVES 4–6   167–250 CALS PER SERVING

Ingredients

2 tbsp olive oil

1 onion, chopped

2 celery stalks, chopped

2 carrots, finely diced

1 x 14oz (400g) can chopped Italian plum tomatoes

1 tbsp tomato paste

1 garlic clove, crushed

salt and black pepper

6¼ cups chicken or vegetable stock

1 x 14oz (400g) can cannellini or red kidney beans, drained

8oz (250g) leeks, trimmed and finely sliced

4oz (125g) Savoy cabbage, finely shredded

2 tbsp arborio (risotto) rice

grated Parmesan cheese to serve

1 Heat the oil in a large saucepan; add the onion, celery, and carrots; and cook gently, stirring, for 5 minutes.

2 Add the tomatoes, tomato paste, and garlic, and season with salt and pepper. Stir, then pour in the stock and bring to a boil over high heat.

3 Cover the pan and lower the heat so the soup is gently simmering. Cook for 15 minutes, stirring occasionally.

4 Add the beans, leeks, cabbage, and rice, and simmer for another 20 minutes. Taste for seasoning.

5 Serve hot, with a bowl of grated Parmesan cheese for everyone to help themselves.

Cook's know-how

If you don't have arborio or any other type of risotto rice, use broken spaghetti instead. You will need 1oz (30g).

TOMATO SOUP

SERVES 6–8   101–134 CALS PER SERVING

Ingredients

2 tbsp butter

2 onions, coarsely chopped

1 garlic clove, crushed

1 tbsp all-purpose flour

5¼ cups vegetable
   or chicken stock

2 x 14oz (400g)
   cans tomatoes

1 bay leaf

salt and black pepper

¼ cup store-bought pesto

half-and-half (optional)
   and fresh basil leaves
   to garnish

1 Melt the butter in a large saucepan, add the onions and garlic, and cook gently, stirring from time to time, for a few minutes until soft but not colored.

2 Add the flour to the pan and cook, stirring constantly, for 1 minute.

3 Pour in the stock, then add the tomatoes and their juice and the bay leaf. Season with salt and pepper. Bring to a boil, cover the pan, and simmer gently for 20 minutes.

4 Remove the bay leaf and discard. Purée the soup in a food processor or blender until smooth.

5 Return the soup to the rinsed-out pan, add the pesto, and heat through. Taste for seasoning.

6 Serve at once, garnished with half-and-half (if you like) and fresh basil leaves.

CLAM CHOWDER

SERVES 4   497 CALS PER SERVING

Ingredients

1lb (500g) fresh clams in
  their shells, cleaned
  (page 15)

1 cup fish stock

3 tbsp butter

1 onion, chopped

3 slices bacon, diced

2 tbsp all-purpose flour

2 potatoes, peeled
  and diced

3 cups milk

1 bay leaf

salt and black pepper

1 Put the clams into a large saucepan, add the fish stock, and bring to a boil. Lower the heat, cover, and cook over medium heat for 5–8 minutes until the clam shells open.

2 Discard any clams that have not opened. Set aside 12 clams in their shells for garnish and keep warm. Remove the remaining clams from their shells. Discard the shells and strain the cooking juices.

3 Melt the butter in a large pan, add the onion, and cook gently for a few minutes until soft but not browned. Add the bacon and the flour and cook, stirring, for 1–2 minutes.

4 Add the potatoes, milk, strained clam juices, and bay leaf to the pan. Bring to a boil, then lower the heat and simmer for 15 minutes. Add the shelled clams and heat gently for about 5 minutes. Remove the bay leaf and discard.

5 Add salt and pepper to taste. Serve hot, garnished with the reserved clams in their shells.

BUTTERNUT SQUASH
soup

SERVES 6   197 CALS PER SERVING

Ingredients

3 small butternut squash,
   about 3½lb (1.7kg)
   total weight

2 tbsp olive oil

grated nutmeg

salt and black pepper

2 tbsp butter

1 large onion,
   coarsely chopped

2 large carrots,
   coarsely chopped

2 large celery stalks,
   coarsely chopped

5–5½ cups vegetable stock

crusty bread to serve

1 Preheat the oven to 400°F (200°C). Cut each squash lengthwise in half, then scoop out and discard the seeds and stringy fibers. Arrange the squash halves cut-side up in a roasting pan just large enough to hold them in a single layer. Drizzle the olive oil over the flesh of the squash and season with nutmeg, salt, and pepper. Pour ⅔ cup cold water into the pan around the squash. Roast in the oven for about 1 hour until tender. Remove from the oven and set aside until cool enough to handle.

2 Meanwhile, melt the butter in a large saucepan and add the chopped vegetables. Cook over high heat for a few minutes until lightly colored, stirring constantly. Pour in the stock, season with salt and pepper, and bring to a boil. Cover and simmer gently for 20 minutes or until the vegetables are tender. Remove from the heat.

3 Scoop the flesh from the squash skins into the soup in the pan, then purée in a food processor or blender until smooth. (If using a food processor, purée the vegetables with a little of the liquid first, then add the remaining liquid and purée again.) Return the soup to the rinsed-out pan, reheat, and taste for seasoning. Serve hot, with crusty bread.

CHICKEN NOODLE
soup

SERVES 6   261 CALS PER SERVING

Ingredients

1lb (500g) chicken thighs

1lb (500g) carrots, sliced

½ head celery, chopped

1 small onion, peeled
 but left whole

2–3 garlic cloves,
 coarsely chopped

a few parsley sprigs

7¼ cups chicken stock

salt and black pepper

4oz (125g) thin noodles

chopped fresh dill to garnish

1 Put the chicken thighs into a large saucepan with the carrots, celery, onion, garlic, and parsley. Pour in the stock and bring to a boil. Using a slotted spoon, skim off the foam that rises to the top of the pan.

2 Lower the heat and season with salt and pepper. Cover and simmer gently for 30 minutes.

3 Skim any fat from the surface of the soup. With a slotted spoon, remove the parsley, onion, and chicken. Discard the parsley. Chop the onion and shred the chicken meat, discarding the skin and bones. Set aside.

4 Break the noodles into 2in (5cm) pieces and drop them into the soup. Bring to a boil, cover, and simmer for about 10 minutes or until tender.

5 Return the onion and chicken to the soup, heat through, and taste for seasoning. Serve hot, garnished with dill.

AVOCADO CAPRESE
salad

SERVES 4   509 CALS PER SERVING

Ingredients

4 beefsteak or slicing
  tomatoes

salt and black pepper

8oz (250g) fresh mozzarella

2 avocados

2 tbsp lemon juice

3–4 tbsp extra virgin
  olive oil

basil sprigs to garnish

1 Slice the tomatoes thinly, put into a bowl, and sprinkle with salt and pepper. Thinly slice the mozzarella.

2 Prepare the avocado (see box, below). Cut the avocados in half lengthwise. Twist to loosen the halves and pull them apart. Remove the pit, score and peel off the skin, then cut the halves crosswise.

3 Cut the avocado quarters into slices lengthwise, then sprinkle with lemon juice to prevent discoloration.

4 Arrange the tomato, mozzarella, and avocado slices attractively on a platter. Drizzle with the extra virgin olive oil and garnish with basil sprigs before serving.

PREPARING AVOCADO

Cut the avocado in half lengthwise around the pit and twist the 2 halves to separate them. Remove the pit. If the avocado is to be mashed, the flesh can simply be scooped out of the skin with a teaspoon. To serve in slices, lightly score the skin into 2 or 3 strips, then peel off the strips of skin and slice the flesh.

SALADE NIÇOISE

SERVES 4   530 CALS PER SERVING

Ingredients

8oz (250g) green beans, cut in half crosswise

salt and black pepper

2 hard-boiled eggs

1 romaine lettuce

½ cucumber, sliced

4 tomatoes, quartered

1 x 7oz (200g) can tuna, drained

1 small yellow onion, very thinly sliced

1 x 2oz (60g) can anchovy fillets, drained

12 pitted black olives

chopped parsley to garnish

Dressing

⅔ cup olive oil

3 tbsp white wine vinegar

1 garlic clove, crushed

½ tsp Dijon mustard

1 Cook the green beans in boiling salted water for 4–5 minutes until just tender. Drain, rinse under cold running water, and drain again.

2 Peel the shells from the eggs, and cut the eggs into wedges lengthwise.

3 Make the dressing: combine the oil, vinegar, garlic, and mustard, and season with salt and pepper.

4 Tear the lettuce leaves into pieces and place on a large serving plate. Arrange the cucumber and beans on top of the lettuce.

5 Arrange the tomatoes and eggs on the serving plate. Coarsely flake the tuna with a fork and place in the middle. Arrange the onion, anchovy fillets, and olives over the tuna. Pour over the dressing, garnish with parsley, and serve at once.

SPINACH
and bacon salad

SERVES 6   436 CALS PER SERVING

Ingredients

1lb (500g) baby spinach leaves, all stems removed

3 large slices of thick-cut white bread, crusts removed

¼ cup sunflower oil

1 garlic clove, crushed

12 slices thick-cut bacon, chopped

4–5 tbsp vinaigrette or blue cheese dressing (see box, below)

salt and black pepper

1 Tear the spinach leaves into large pieces and place them in a salad bowl.

2 Make the croutons: cut the bread into small cubes. Heat the sunflower oil in a frying pan, add the garlic, and cook for 1 minute. Add the bread cubes and cook, stirring, for 1–2 minutes until golden and crisp. Lift out the croutons and drain on paper towels.

3 Add the bacon to the pan and fry for 5 minutes or until crisp. Lift out and drain on paper towels.

4 Sprinkle the bacon over the spinach. Spoon the dressing over the salad, season with salt and pepper, and toss gently. Scatter the croutons over the salad and serve at once.

VINAIGRETTE DRESSING

Put 6 tbsp olive oil, 2 tbsp white wine vinegar, 1 tbsp lemon juice, 1 tbsp Dijon mustard, ¼ tsp granulated sugar, and salt and pepper to taste into a screw-top jar. Shake until combined. This makes ¾ cup.

BLUE CHEESE DRESSING

Put ¾ cup each of mayonnaise and sour cream into a bowl with 3oz (90g) mashed blue cheese, 1 tsp white wine vinegar, 1 crushed garlic clove, and black pepper to taste. Whisk until smooth.

WALDORF SALAD

SERVES 4   469 CALS PER SERVING

Ingredients

1lb (500g) crisp red-skinned
  apples, cored and diced

juice of ½ lemon

4 celery stalks, thickly sliced

⅔ cup mayonnaise
  (see box, below)

salt and black pepper

¾ cup walnut pieces,
  coarsely chopped

chopped parsley to garnish

1 Put the diced apples into a bowl, pour the lemon juice over the top, and stir to coat thoroughly to prevent discoloration. Transfer to a salad bowl and add the celery.

2 Spoon the mayonnaise over the salad, season with salt and pepper, and toss gently to mix. Cover and chill until required. Stir in the walnut pieces and garnish with chopped parsley just before serving.

TRADITIONAL MAYONNAISE

Put a bowl on a kitchen towel to steady it. Add 2 large egg yolks, 1 tsp Dijon mustard, and salt and pepper to taste, and beat together with a balloon whisk until the egg yolks have thickened slightly.

Whisk in ⅔ cup olive or sunflower oil, or a mixture of the two, just a drop at a time at first, whisking until the mixture is thick. Stir in 2 tsp white wine vinegar or lemon juice. Check the seasoning, adding sugar to taste if you like. Serve at once, or chill. This makes ¾ cup.

CAESAR SALAD

SERVES 4   421 CALS PER SERVING

Ingredients

Croutons

3 large slices of thick-cut white bread, crusts removed

¼ cup olive oil

1 garlic clove, crushed

For the salad

1 head romaine lettuce

¼ cup olive oil

2 tbsp lemon juice

salt and black pepper

2 hard-boiled eggs, peeled

1oz (30g) Parmesan cheese, coarsely grated

1   Make the croutons: cut the bread into small cubes. Heat the olive oil in a frying pan, add the garlic, and cook for 1 minute. Add the bread cubes and cook, stirring, for 1–2 minutes until crisp. Lift out and drain on paper towels.

2   Tear the lettuce leaves into bite-sized pieces and put them into a salad bowl. Whisk the olive oil and lemon juice, season with salt and pepper, and toss with the leaves.

3   Cut the hard-boiled eggs into quarters, and add to the salad. Add the croutons and Parmesan cheese and toss gently. Serve at once.

VARIATION

CAESAR SALAD with anchovies

Coarsely chop 6 canned anchovy fillets and add to the salad with the hard-boiled eggs in step 3.

Cook's know-how

If you prefer a lighter salad, you can toast the bread to make the croutons rather than frying it in oil.

CRUNCHY ASIAN
salad

SERVES 6   141 CALS PER SERVING

Ingredients

1 head iceberg or
   romaine lettuce

6oz (175g) bean sprouts

6 scallions, thinly sliced
   on a diagonal

1 green bell pepper, halved,
   seeded, and thinly sliced

2 tbsp toasted
   sesame seeds

Dressing

3 tbsp sunflower or olive oil

1 tsp sesame oil

1 tbsp white wine vinegar

1 garlic clove, crushed

½in (1cm) piece of fresh
   ginger, peeled and grated

½ tsp granulated sugar,
   or to taste

salt and black pepper

1 Tear the lettuce leaves into bite-sized pieces. Put the lettuce, bean sprouts, scallions, and bell pepper into a salad bowl and mix together.

2 Make the dressing: combine the oils, vinegar, garlic, and ginger, and season to taste with sugar, salt, and pepper.

3 Toss the salad with the dressing, sprinkle with the sesame seeds, and serve.

PREPARING BELL PEPPERS

Cut around the stalk and the core. Twist and pull them out in one piece.

Cut the bell pepper in half. Scrape out the fleshy white ribs and the seeds.

POTATO SALAD

SERVES 8   357 CALS PER SERVING

Ingredients

2lb (1kg) new potatoes, scrubbed

salt and black pepper

1 small yellow onion, very finely chopped

¼ cup vinaigrette dressing (page 48)

1 cup mayonnaise (page 49), or less if preferred

2 tbsp snipped fresh chives, plus extra to garnish

1 Put the potatoes into a large saucepan of boiling salted water and simmer for 15–20 minutes until tender. Drain the potatoes thoroughly. Cut them into even-sized pieces.

2 Put the potatoes into a large salad bowl and add the chopped onion.

3 While the potatoes are still warm, spoon the vinaigrette dressing over them and then toss gently to mix all the ingredients thoroughly.

4 Add the mayonnaise and the chives and mix together gently. Add salt and pepper to taste, cover, and chill for about 30 minutes (the salad is best served not too cold). Garnish with extra chives before serving.

GREEK SALAD

SERVES 4–6   335–503 CALS PER SERVING

Ingredients

4 beefsteak or
  slicing tomatoes

1 cucumber, sliced

8oz (250g) feta
  cheese, diced

24 black olives, pitted

½ cup extra virgin olive oil

¼ cup lemon juice

salt and black pepper

2 tbsp chopped fresh
  oregano or flat-leaf parsley

1 Halve the tomatoes lengthwise, cut out the cores, and cut each half into 4 wedges.

2 Put the tomatoes into a large salad bowl and add the cucumber, feta cheese, and olives.

3 Spoon over the olive oil and lemon juice and add salt and black pepper to taste (do not use too much salt as feta is a salty cheese), then toss gently to mix.

4 Sprinkle the salad with the oregano or parsley before serving.

SPICY CHICKEN
wings

SERVES 4–6   137–206 CALS PER SERVING

Ingredients

1lb (500g) chicken wings

2 tbsp sunflower oil

1 tsp lemon juice

1 tbsp paprika

1 tsp ground cumin

½ tsp oregano

½ tsp mild chili powder

black pepper

To serve

½ red bell pepper, cut into
  strips

½ head celery, cut into
  sticks, plus leaves

blue cheese dressing
  (page 48)

parsley sprigs to garnish

1 Cut the chicken wings in half and put the pieces in a shallow dish.

2 In a large bowl, combine the oil, lemon juice, paprika, cumin, oregano, chili powder, and black pepper. Brush the mixture over the chicken, cover, and let marinate at room temperature for at least 1 hour. Preheat the oven to 400°F (200°C).

3 Line a large baking sheet with foil and place a rack on top. Lay the chicken wings in a single layer on the rack and cook for 40 minutes, or until browned, sizzling, and crispy.

4 Remove the chicken from the rack and drain on paper towels. Serve with red bell pepper strips, celery sticks, and blue cheese dressing, and garnish with parsley.

SPICED
meatballs

SERVES 8   481 CALS PER SERVING

Ingredients

Sesame dip

2 tbsp soy sauce

2 tbsp sesame oil

1 tbsp rice wine vinegar or sherry

1 scallion, thinly sliced

1 tbsp sesame seeds, toasted

For the meatballs

2lb (1kg) lean ground beef

1 small onion, grated

2 garlic cloves, crushed

1 large egg, beaten

¾ cup fresh bread crumbs

2 tbsp tomato paste

2 tbsp paprika

2 tbsp chopped fresh cilantro

salt and black pepper

3 tbsp olive oil for frying

chopped parsley to garnish

crudités to serve

1 Make the sesame dip: whisk all the ingredients together and set aside.

2 Combine the meatball ingredients in a bowl. Using your hands, roll the mixture into little balls.

3 Heat the oil in a frying pan and cook the meatballs, in batches, over medium heat for 5 minutes or until browned, firm, and cooked through. Garnish and serve warm with the sesame dip and crudités.

NACHOS GRANDE

SERVES 6   396 CALS PER SERVING

Ingredients

2 tbsp sunflower oil

1 onion, finely chopped

½ green bell
   pepper, chopped

3 garlic cloves, crushed

1 x 8oz (250g) can
   chopped tomatoes

½–1 fresh jalapeño chile,
   halved, seeded, and
   finely chopped

½ tsp chili powder

½ tsp paprika

1 x 14oz (400g) can
   refried beans

1 x 3oz (90g) package
   tortilla chips

¼ tsp ground cumin

6oz (175g) Cheddar
   cheese, grated

extra paprika to garnish

1   Preheat the oven to 400°F (200°C). Heat the oil in a frying pan; add the onion, green bell pepper, and garlic; and cook gently, stirring occasionally, for 5 minutes or until softened.

2   Add the tomatoes and chile and cook over medium heat for another 5 minutes, or until most of the liquid has evaporated.

3   Stir in the chili powder and paprika and cook for 3 minutes, then add the refried beans, breaking them up with a fork. Add ⅓ cup water and cook, stirring from time to time, for 8–10 minutes, until the mixture thickens.

4   Spoon the beans into a baking dish, arrange the tortilla chips around the edge, and sprinkle with cumin. Sprinkle the cheese over the beans and tortilla chips.

5   Bake for 15–20 minutes until the cheese has melted. Sprinkle paprika on top before serving.

HUMMUS

SERVES 6   150 CALS PER SERVING

Ingredients

2 x 14oz (400g) cans
  chickpeas, drained

2–3 garlic cloves,
  coarsely chopped

1 tbsp tahini paste,
  or to taste

3 tbsp olive oil, or to taste

juice of 1 lemon, or to taste

salt and black pepper

1 Purée the chickpeas, garlic, tahini paste, oil, and lemon juice in a food processor or blender until smooth.

2 Add salt and pepper to taste and more oil, tahini, and lemon juice if you think it needs it, then purée again.

3 Spoon into dishes and level the surface. If you like, garnish with rosemary, red bell pepper, and olives.

CHOPPING GARLIC

Set the flat side of a knife on top of the clove and crush it lightly. Peel off the skin.

With a sharp chef's knife, chop the crushed garlic clove finely.

SHRIMP SALAD

SERVES 4 338 CALS PER SERVING

Ingredients

⅔ cup mayonnaise

2 tbsp creamed horseradish

1 tbsp lemon juice

1 tsp Worcestershire sauce

1 tsp tomato paste

¼ tsp granulated sugar

a few drops of
  hot pepper sauce

black pepper

8oz (250g) peeled,
  cooked shrimp

lettuce leaves to serve

thin lemon wedges, parsley
  sprigs, and 4 large cooked
  shrimp in their shells
  to garnish

1 Make the dressing: in a medium bowl, combine the mayonnaise, creamed horseradish, lemon juice, Worcestershire sauce, tomato paste, granulated sugar, and hot pepper sauce, and season well with black pepper.

2 Add the peeled, cooked shrimp and stir to coat with the dressing.

3 Line 4 individual glass serving bowls with the lettuce leaves and top with the shrimp mixture. Garnish each serving with a thin lemon wedge, a parsley sprig, and a large shrimp.

SUN-DRIED TOMATO
crostini

SERVES 8   165 CALS PER SERVING

Ingredients

1 baguette

2 garlic cloves, crushed

about 3 tbsp olive oil

4 sun-dried tomatoes in oil

2 tbsp butter

salt and black pepper

12 pitted black olives,
   chopped

¼ tsp fresh rosemary,
   chopped

1 Preheat the oven to 350°F (180°C). Cut the baguette into 24 thin slices and arrange them on 2 baking sheets. Add the garlic to the olive oil, then brush about half of the mixture onto the slices of bread. Bake for 10 minutes.

2 Remove the baking sheets from the oven, turn the slices of bread over, brush with a little more garlic oil, and bake for another 10 minutes or until crisp and golden. Let cool.

3 Dry the sun-dried tomatoes with a paper towel and cut them into pieces. Put the tomato and butter in the small bowl of a food processor and work until finely chopped (or pound them with a mortar and pestle). Season with salt and pepper to taste.

4 Spread the sun-dried tomato paste over the crostini, arrange the chopped olives on top, and sprinkle with rosemary.

Pizza tartlets

These mini pizzas, with their traditional flavors, make a tasty appetizer to serve with predinner drinks. They will also serve 4 people as a light lunch.

PIZZA
tartlets

MAKES 12   198 CALS EACH

Ingredients

Tartlet dough

1⅓ cups all-purpose flour

6 tbsp butter

For the topping

⅓ cup store-bought red
  or green pesto

1¼ cups ripe tomatoes,
  finely chopped

2–3 garlic cloves, crushed

9 black olives, pitted
  and quartered

4oz (125g) Fontina or
  mozzarella cheese, grated

2–3 tbsp grated
  Parmesan cheese

2 tsp chopped fresh
  marjoram

1 Make the dough: rub the flour and butter together in a bowl with your fingertips. Add enough cold water (about 2 tablespoons) to bind to a soft dough. Wrap in plastic wrap and chill for 30 minutes.

2 Preheat the oven to 400°F (200°C). Make the tartlet shells (see box, below).

3 Spread the pesto in the tartlet shells, then fill the shells with the tomatoes, garlic, black olives, and Fontina cheese.

4 Sprinkle the grated Parmesan cheese over the tartlets, covering the edges as well as the filling. Sprinkle the chopped marjoram on top.

5 Bake the tartlets for 20–30 minutes until the edges are a golden brown and the cheese topping has melted and become crispy. Serve the tartlets warm or cold.

MAKING TARTLET SHELLS

Sprinkle the work surface with flour, then roll out the tartlet dough until ⅛–¼in (3–6mm) thick.

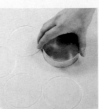
Cut out 12 rounds from the dough, using a 4in (10cm) pastry cutter or the rim of a glass or saucer.

Fold up the edges of the rounds to form rims; put the rounds on a baking sheet.

MAIN DISHES

PROVENÇAL-STYLE
roast chicken

SERVES 6   **547 CALS PER SERVING**

Ingredients

1 large onion,
  cut into wedges

2 large carrots,
  peeled and sliced

4oz (125g) whole
  button mushrooms

3 garlic cloves, peeled

1 cup dry white wine

1½ cups chicken stock

3½lb (1.7kg) chicken, with
  any giblets removed

1 x 14oz (400g) can
  chopped tomatoes

1 tbsp tomato paste

salt and black pepper

chopped parsley to garnish

1 Preheat the oven to 400°F (200°C). Arrange the onion wedges, carrot slices, whole mushrooms, and garlic cloves in a single layer in a roasting pan and pour in the wine and stock.

2 Place the chicken breast-side up on a small roasting rack and place in the middle of the roasting pan on top of the vegetables. Roast for 1½ hours or until the chicken is tender and done (page 12).

3 Remove the chicken from the pan, transfer to a large warmed serving dish, and keep warm.

4 Make the sauce: add the chopped tomatoes and tomato paste to the vegetables in the pan, stir well, and return to the oven for 5 minutes or until hot.

5 Carefully pour the contents of the pan into a food processor or blender and purée until smooth. Season with salt and pepper.

6 Pour the sauce over the roast chicken, garnish with chopped parsley, and serve at once.

CHICKEN
cacciatore

SERVES 4   540 CALS PER SERVING

Ingredients

8 small chicken portions
(4 legs and 4 breasts
or 8 thighs)

all-purpose flour for dusting

salt and black pepper

3–4 tbsp olive oil

3oz (90g) thick-cut bacon or
pancetta, cut into strips

1 large onion, chopped

1 small green bell pepper,
halved, seeded, and diced

2 garlic cloves, crushed

8oz (250g) mushrooms,
quartered

½ cup red or white wine

1 x 14oz (400g) can
chopped tomatoes

⅓ cup tomato paste

2 tsp chopped fresh sage

¼ cup chopped parsley

grated zest of 1 lemon

2 tbsp capers, chopped

fresh sage leaves to garnish

1 Preheat the oven to 350°F (180°C). Lightly dust the chicken pieces with flour seasoned with salt and pepper and shake off any excess.

2 Heat half of the oil in a large frying pan, add the bacon or pancetta and chicken, and cook for 10–12 minutes until browned all over. Transfer to a Dutch oven with a slotted spoon, then pour off the fat from the frying pan.

3 Heat the remaining oil in the frying pan; add the onion, green bell pepper, and half of the garlic; and cook gently, stirring, for 5 minutes until soft but not browned. Transfer to the Dutch oven with a slotted spoon. Add the mushrooms and cook for 2 minutes. Add to the pot.

4 Pour the wine into the frying pan and boil until reduced to about ¼ cup. Add to the pot with the tomatoes, tomato paste, and the sage. Cover and cook in the oven for 45 minutes or until the chicken is tender when pierced with a fork.

5 Combine the remaining garlic with the chopped parsley, lemon zest, and capers. Stir into the pot and taste for seasoning. Serve hot with mashed potatoes and garnished with sage leaves.

CHICKEN
pot pie

SERVES 6   508 CALS PER SERVING

Ingredients

2lb (1kg) chicken

5¼ cups chicken stock

1 onion, quartered

1 celery stalk, thickly sliced

peeled zest and juice
   of 1 lemon

2 carrots

2 waxy potatoes, peeled
   and cut into quarters

3 tbsp butter

⅓ cup all-purpose flour,
   plus extra for dusting

salt and black pepper

4oz (125g) frozen peas

6oz (175g) pie dough

beaten egg yolk for glazing

Special equipment

1-quart (1-liter) pie dish

1 Put the chicken, stock, onion, celery, and lemon zest into a large saucepan. Bring to a boil, cover, and simmer for 30 minutes.

2 Add the carrots and potatoes, cover, and simmer for about 20 minutes or until the vegetables are cooked and the chicken is just tender. Remove the vegetables from the liquid and set aside. Let the chicken cool in the liquid.

3 Remove the meat from the chicken and cut into bite-sized pieces, discarding the skin and bones. Dice the vegetables.

4 Skim the fat from the cooking liquid, then bring 2½ cups to a boil. Melt the butter in another pan, add the flour, and cook, stirring occasionally, for 1 minute. Stir in the hot stock, whisking until it comes to a boil and thickens. Add the lemon juice and season with salt and pepper.

5 Stir the chicken, diced vegetables, and peas into the sauce, then let cool. Preheat the oven to 375°F (190°C).

6 On a lightly floured work surface, roll out the dough. Invert the pie dish onto the dough and use a small knife to cut around the edge, keeping the blade close to the dish. Reserve all trimmings. Transfer the cold filling to the pie dish and top with the rolled-out dough. Press the dough with your fingertips onto the rim of the pie dish. Crimp the edge of the dough with a fork.

7 Brush the dough with the beaten egg yolk, making a lattice pattern. Cut decorative shapes from the reserved dough trimmings with a pastry cutter. Arrange on top of the pie and glaze the shapes with the beaten egg yolk.

8 Bake for 30 minutes or until the top is crisp and golden brown. Serve hot.

TEX-MEX
chicken

SERVES 6   659 CALS PER SERVING

Ingredients

Marinade

¼ cup olive oil

¼ cup orange juice

1 tsp ground cumin

For the chicken

4 skinless, boneless
  chicken breasts

2 avocados

2 tbsp lime juice

1 red onion, finely chopped

For the salsa

1lb (500g) tomatoes,
  chopped

1 small red onion,
  finely chopped

3 tbsp olive oil

2 tbsp lime juice

3 tbsp chopped
  fresh cilantro

2 garlic cloves, crushed

1 fresh jalapeño chile,
  halved, seeded, and
  chopped

salt, to taste

1 Mix the marinade ingredients together. Make several diagonal slashes in each chicken breast, then put the chicken in a nonmetallic dish. Pour the marinade over the chicken. Cover and marinate in the refrigerator for at least 30 minutes, or overnight.

2 Make the salsa: combine the tomatoes, onion, oil, lime juice, cilantro, garlic, chile, and salt to taste. Cover and chill until ready to serve.

3 Remove the chicken from the marinade, and put under a hot broiler, 4in (10cm) from the heat. Broil for 3–5 minutes on each side, depending on the size of the chicken, until the juices run clear when the chicken is pierced.

4 Meanwhile, halve, pit, and peel the avocados (page 44). Slice lengthwise and brush with lime juice.

5 Thinly slice the chicken breasts, following the slashes made before marinating. Arrange the avocado and chicken slices on plates and sprinkle the chopped red onion around the edges. Spoon a little of the salsa into the middle of each serving and serve the remainder separately.

COQ AU VIN

SERVES 4   531 CALS PER SERVING

Ingredients

2 tbsp butter

1 tbsp sunflower oil

3lb (1.5kg) chicken, cut into 8
   serving pieces

4oz (125g) thick-cut bacon,
   cut into strips

8 small shallots or
   pickling onions

8oz (250g) button
   mushrooms

3 tbsp all-purpose flour

2½ cups red wine

1¼ cups chicken stock

1 bouquet garni (page 13)

1 large garlic clove, crushed

salt and black pepper

2 tbsp chopped parsley
   to garnish

1 Melt the butter with the oil in a large Dutch oven. Add the chicken and cook for 10–12 minutes until browned all over. Lift out and let drain on paper towels.

2 Spoon off any excess fat, then add the bacon, shallots or onions, and mushrooms. Cook over high heat, stirring, until golden brown.

3 Lift the mixture out of the pan with a slotted spoon and let drain thoroughly on paper towels. Preheat the oven to 350°F (180°C).

4 Add the flour to the pan and cook for 3–5 minutes, stirring constantly until lightly browned. Reduce the wine in a separate pan until it reduces to 1½ cups. Gradually pour in the stock, then the wine, stirring until smooth.

5 Return the chicken, bacon, shallots or onions, and mushrooms to the pot and add the bouquet garni and garlic. Season with salt and pepper. Bring to a boil, cover, and bake in the oven for 45 minutes or until the chicken is tender when pierced with a fork.

6 Sprinkle the chicken with the chopped parsley and serve hot.

Coq au vin

A traditional French dish that became a popular dinner party staple in the 1960s.

JERK CHICKEN

SERVES 4   304 CALS PER SERVING

Ingredients

Jerk paste

3 tbsp lime juice

2 tbsp dark rum

2 tbsp sunflower oil

4 scallions, coarsely chopped

1–2 fresh jalapeño chiles,
halved, seeded, and
coarsely chopped

2 garlic cloves,
coarsely chopped

1 tbsp ground allspice

2 tsp fresh thyme leaves

salt and black pepper

For the chicken

4 chicken legs or drumsticks

To serve

chopped fresh thyme

grilled pineapple rings

1 Make the jerk paste: purée the ingredients in a food processor
with a pinch each of salt and pepper.

2 Put the chicken pieces in a nonmetallic dish and brush them all
over with the jerk paste. Cover and marinate in the refrigerator
for at least 30 minutes, or overnight.

3 Put the chicken on a hot grill, or under a hot broiler 4in (10cm)
from the heat. Cook for 10 minutes on each side or until the
juices run clear when the chicken is pierced.

4 Serve the chicken hot or cold, sprinkled with thyme, and
accompanied by grilled pineapple rings, if you like.

THAI CHICKEN
with water chestnuts

SERVES 4   272 CALS PER SERVING

Ingredients

4 skinless, boneless chicken
breasts, cut into 1in
(2.5cm) pieces

3 tbsp sunflower oil

2 garlic cloves, crushed

1in (2.5cm) piece of fresh
ginger, peeled and grated

½–1 fresh jalapeño chile,
halved, seeded, and
chopped

1 tsp soy sauce, or more
to taste

½ tsp sugar

salt and black pepper

2½ cups chicken stock

1 stem of lemongrass,
bruised

grated zest of 1 lime

1 x 7oz (200g) can water
chestnuts, drained,
rinsed, and sliced

1 small bunch of fresh
cilantro, coarsely chopped

lime wedges, sliced
scallions, and peanuts
to garnish

1 Put the chicken into a dish and add the oil, garlic, ginger, chile,
soy sauce, and sugar. Season with black pepper, stir well, then
let stand for a few minutes.

2 Heat a nonstick wok or frying pan, add the chicken mixture,
in batches if necessary, and stir-fry for 2–3 minutes or until
lightly browned.

3 Pour in the stock, add any marinade left in the dish, then
add the lemongrass, lime zest, water chestnuts, and cilantro.
Continue stir-frying for a few minutes more until the chicken is tender.

4 Taste the stir-fry and add more soy sauce, if you like. Serve at once,
garnished with lime wedges, scallion slices, and peanuts.

CHOPPING FRESH GINGER

With a small knife, peel off the skin. Slice the ginger
across the fibrous grain.

Set the flat of a knife on top of the slices and crush.
Chop the slices.

FRAGRANT CHICKEN
curry with almonds

SERVES 4   527 CALS PER SERVING

Ingredients

2 cloves

2 tsp cumin seeds

seeds of 4 cardamom pods

1 tsp garam masala

pinch of cayenne pepper

2 tbsp sunflower oil

4 skinless, boneless chicken breasts

1 large onion, finely chopped

2 garlic cloves, crushed

1in (2.5cm) piece of fresh ginger, peeled and finely grated

salt and black pepper

1¼ cups chicken stock

¾ cup half-and-half

1 x 5½oz (150g) carton full-fat yogurt

golden raisins and whole almonds, blanched, shredded, and toasted (see box, below), and cilantro to garnish

1 Crush the cloves in a mortar and pestle with the cumin and cardamom seeds. Mix in the garam masala and cayenne.

2 Heat the oil in a Dutch oven. Add the chicken breasts and cook for 2–3 minutes on each side until golden. Remove with a slotted spoon and let drain on paper towels.

3 Add the onion, garlic, and ginger to the pan and cook gently, stirring occasionally, for a few minutes until just beginning to soften. Add the spice mixture and season with salt and pepper, then stir over high heat for 1 minute.

4 Return the chicken to the Dutch oven. Pour in the stock and bring to a boil. Cover and simmer gently for 15 minutes or until the chicken is tender.

5 Stir in the half-and-half and yogurt, heat through very gently, then taste for seasoning.

6 Serve hot with boiled rice. Sprinkle with the golden raisins, toasted shredded almonds, and a few torn cilantro leaves.

PREPARE THE ALMONDS

Immerse the almonds in a bowl of boiling water. When cool enough, squeeze the almonds between your fingers to slide and pull off the skins.

Slice the almonds in half lengthwise. Cut the halves into shreds and place on a baking sheet.

Toast in a preheated oven at 350°F (180°C), stirring occasionally to ensure even color, for 8–10 minutes until lightly browned.

SWEET AND SOUR
chicken

SERVES 4–6   458–305 CALS PER SERVING

Ingredients

1lb (500g) skinless, boneless chicken breasts, cut into 1in (2.5cm) pieces

2 tbsp dark soy sauce

1 tbsp Chinese rice wine or dry sherry

1 x 8oz (250g) can pineapple chunks in natural juice, drained and juice reserved

2 tbsp cornstarch

3 tbsp sunflower oil

1 green bell pepper, halved, seeded, and cut into bite-sized pieces

1 red bell pepper, halved, seeded, and cut into bite-sized pieces

1 celery stalk, thickly sliced

1 onion, cut into bite-sized chunks

¼ cup ketchup

8oz (250g) canned lychees, drained and juice reserved

salt and black pepper

chopped fresh cilantro to garnish (optional)

1 Toss the chicken pieces in a large bowl with the soy sauce and rice wine or sherry. Cover and marinate in the refrigerator for at least 30 minutes.

2 Meanwhile, add enough water to the reserved pineapple juice to make 1 cup and blend with the cornstarch. Set aside.

3 Heat the oil in a wok or large frying pan, add the chicken, in batches if necessary, and stir-fry for 3–4 minutes until golden all over. Lift out with a slotted spoon.

4 Add the green and red bell peppers, celery, and onion to the wok and stir-fry for about 5 minutes.

5 Add the cornstarch and pineapple juice mixture, ketchup, and reserved lychee juice to the wok and cook for 3–5 minutes until thickened.

6 Return the chicken to the wok with the lychees and pineapple chunks and heat through. Season with salt and pepper and serve at once garnished with fresh cilantro, if desired.

CHICKEN
with sage and orange

SERVES 6   435 CALS PER SERVING

Ingredients

Marinade

1¼ cups orange juice

1 tbsp light soy sauce

2 garlic cloves, crushed

2 tbsp chopped fresh sage

½in (1cm) piece of fresh
   ginger, peeled and grated

salt and black pepper

For the chicken

6 boneless chicken breasts,
   with the skin on

1 tbsp all-purpose flour

orange segments and fresh
   sage leaves to garnish

1 Make the marinade: combine the orange juice, soy sauce, garlic, sage, ginger, and salt and pepper. Toss the chicken in the marinade, cover, and let marinate in the refrigerator for 20–30 minutes. Meanwhile, preheat the oven to 375°F (190°C).

2 Reserve the marinade and arrange the chicken breasts, skin-side up, in a large roasting pan.

3 Roast the chicken in the oven for 10 minutes. Pour the reserved marinade over the chicken and continue roasting for 10 minutes or until the chicken is cooked through.

4 Remove the chicken with a slotted spoon and arrange on a warmed platter. Cover and keep warm.

5 Pour all but 2 tablespoons of the marinade into a measuring cup and reserve. Add the flour to the marinade remaining in the roasting pan and mix to a smooth paste.

6 Put the roasting pan on the stove top and cook, stirring, for 1 minute. Gradually stir in the reserved marinade. Bring to a boil, simmer for 2 minutes, and taste for seasoning. Strain, pour a little around the chicken breasts, and garnish with the orange segments and fresh sage. Accompany with boiled new potatoes and broccoli. Serve the remaining sauce separately.

CHICKEN
cordon bleu

SERVES 4   602 CALS PER SERVING

Ingredients

4 skinless, boneless
  chicken breasts

4 thin slices of
  Gruyère cheese

4 thin slices of cooked ham

salt and black pepper

1 large egg, beaten

1½ cups fresh white
  bread crumbs

2 tbsp butter

3 tbsp sunflower oil

1 With a sharp knife, cut each chicken breast horizontally, leaving it attached at one side.

2 Open out each chicken breast, place between 2 sheets of wax paper, and pound to an ⅛in (3mm) thickness with a rolling pin. Fill and fold the chicken breasts (see box, below).

3 Dip each folded chicken breast into the beaten egg, then dip each breast into the bread crumbs, making sure each one is evenly coated. Cover and chill for 15 minutes.

4 Melt the butter with the sunflower oil in a large frying pan. When the butter is foaming, add the chicken breasts and cook for 10 minutes on each side or until the bread crumb coating is crisp and golden and the chicken is cooked through. Remove the chicken breasts with a slotted spoon and drain thoroughly on paper towels. Cut into ½in (1cm) slices and serve at once.

FOLDING THE CHICKEN

Place 1 slice of cheese and 1 slice of ham on half of each chicken breast, season with salt and pepper, and fold the breast over to cover the filling.

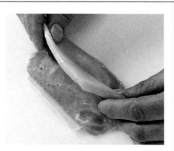

TURKEY
schnitzel

SERVES 4   394 CALS PER SERVING

Ingredients

3 tbsp all-purpose flour

salt and black pepper

1 large egg, beaten

½ cup fresh bread crumbs

4 x 6oz (175g) turkey
breast cutlets

2 tbsp sunflower oil

3 tsp butter

lemon slices and chopped
parsley to garnish

1 Sprinkle the flour onto a plate and season generously with salt
and pepper. Pour the beaten egg onto another plate and sprinkle
the bread crumbs onto a third plate.

2 Coat each cutlet with the seasoned flour, shaking off any
excess. Dip each floured cutlet into the beaten egg, then
dip into the bread crumbs.

3 With a sharp knife, score the cutlets in a crisscross pattern.
Cover and chill in the refrigerator for 30 minutes.

4 Heat the oil with the butter in a large frying pan. When the butter
is foaming, add the cutlets and cook over high heat until golden on
both sides.

5 Lower the heat and cook for 10 minutes or until the cutlets are
tender. Test the cutlets by piercing with a fine skewer: the juices
should run clear.

6 Lift the cutlets out of the pan and drain on paper towels.
Garnish with lemon slices and chopped parsley and serve at once.

Cook's know-how

If you can't find turkey breast
cutlets, buy breast fillets. Put
them between 2 sheets of plastic
wrap, and pound with the bottom
of a saucepan until they are about
¼in (5mm) thick.

TURKEY
and lemon stir-fry

SERVES 4   342 CALS PER SERVING

Ingredients

Marinade

½ cup dry white wine

grated zest and juice
  of 1 large lemon

2 tbsp olive oil

salt and black pepper

For the turkey

1¼lb (550g) turkey breast
  fillets, cut diagonally into
  1in (2.5cm) strips

12oz (350g) zucchini

1 large green bell pepper

1 tbsp olive oil

8oz (250g) canned
  baby corn

chopped parsley and lemon
  twists to garnish

1 Make the marinade: combine the wine, lemon zest and juice, and oil, and season with pepper. Toss the turkey strips in the marinade, cover, and marinate in the refrigerator for at least 30 minutes.

2 Slice the zucchini thickly on a diagonal. Halve the green bell pepper and remove the seeds, then cut the pepper halves into long thin strips.

3 Heat the oil in a wok; add the zucchini, baby corn, and green bell pepper; and stir-fry over high heat for 2 minutes. Remove with a slotted spoon and keep warm.

4 Remove the turkey strips from the marinade, reserving the marinade. Add the turkey to the wok and stir-fry over high heat for 5 minutes or until golden.

5 Pour the reserved marinade over the turkey and cook for 3 minutes or until tender. Return the vegetables to the wok and heat through. Taste for seasoning. Serve at once, garnished with parsley and lemon twists.

TURKEY MOLE

SERVES 6   334 CALS PER SERVING

Ingredients

Mole sauce

1 x 14oz (400g) can chopped tomatoes

1 small onion, coarsely chopped

²⁄₃ cup blanched almonds

2 tbsp raisins (optional)

¾oz (20g) bittersweet chocolate, coarsely chopped

1 garlic clove

1 tbsp sesame seeds

1 tbsp hot chili powder

1 tsp ground cinnamon

½ tsp ground cloves

½ tsp ground coriander

½ tsp ground cumin

¼ tsp ground anise (optional)

For the turkey

2 tbsp sunflower oil

1½lb (675g) turkey pieces

1¼ cups turkey or chicken stock

salt and black pepper

1 Make the mole sauce: put the tomatoes, onion, almonds, raisins (if using), chocolate, garlic, sesame seeds, chili powder, cinnamon, cloves, coriander, cumin, anise (if using), and ¼ cup water into a food processor and process briefly.

2 Heat the sunflower oil in a large saucepan, add the turkey pieces, and cook over high heat for about 5 minutes until golden on all sides.

3 Add the mole sauce mixture and cook, stirring, for 2 minutes. Pour in the stock and bring to a boil. Cover and simmer very gently for 40 minutes or until the turkey is tender. Season with salt and pepper before serving.

Cook's know-how

If you would rather not use the almonds, you can use 2 tbsp all-purpose flour to thicken the sauce instead.

ASIAN DUCK
with ginger

SERVES 4   445 CALS PER SERVING

Ingredients

Marinade

¾ cup orange juice

3 tbsp dark soy sauce

1 tbsp sesame oil

1 tbsp Chinese rice wine
or dry sherry

1 tbsp honey

2in (5cm) piece of fresh
ginger, peeled
and grated

1 garlic clove, crushed

salt and black pepper

For the duck

4 x 8–10oz (250–300g)
skinless duck breasts

1 tbsp sunflower oil

8 ears baby corn

bean sprouts and 1 tbsp
toasted sesame seeds
to garnish

1 Make the marinade: in a large bowl, combine the orange juice,
soy sauce, sesame oil, rice wine or sherry, honey, fresh ginger,
and garlic, then season with salt and pepper.

2 With a sharp knife, make several diagonal slashes in each duck breast
(page 90). Pour the marinade over the duck breasts, turn them over,
then cover and marinate in the refrigerator for about 30 minutes.

3 Lift the duck breasts out of the marinade, reserving the marinade.
Heat the oil in a large frying pan, add the duck breasts, and cook
over high heat, turning frequently, for 10–12 minutes until tender.
Add the marinade and simmer for 2–3 minutes until slightly reduced.

4 Drain the baby corn, then make lengthwise cuts in each one, leaving
them attached at the stem.

5 To serve, slice each duck breast and arrange on 4 individual plates.
Spoon the hot sauce over the duck, add the corn, then garnish with
bean sprouts and the toasted sesame seeds. Serve hot.

DUCK BREASTS
with red wine sauce

SERVES 4   906 CALS PER SERVING

Ingredients

Marinade

5 garlic cloves, sliced

2 tbsp balsamic vinegar

1 tbsp chopped fresh
  rosemary

For the duck

4 x 8–10oz (250–300g)
  duck breasts, with
  the skin left on

½ cup beef stock

½ cup red wine

1 tsp tomato paste

1 tsp lemon juice

3 tsp butter

salt and black pepper

1 tbsp chopped fresh
  rosemary to garnish

1 Make the marinade: in a bowl, combine the garlic, vinegar, and
rosemary. Score the duck breasts (see box, below), and put them,
skin-side down, in a shallow dish. Spoon the marinade over the top.
Chill for 30 minutes.

2 Put the duck breasts skin-side down with the marinade in a frying
pan and cook for 5–7 minutes. Turn and cook for another 5 minutes.
Remove from the pan and keep warm.

3 Spoon any excess fat from the frying pan. Add the stock and wine
and boil over high heat until reduced to a dark glaze, then add the
tomato paste and lemon juice.

4 Remove from heat and whisk in the butter, letting it thicken the
sauce as it melts. Taste for seasoning.

5 Slice the duck and arrange on warmed plates. Spoon the sauce
around the duck, sprinkle with the chopped rosemary, and
serve with boiled potatoes and green beans.

SCORING AND SEASONING THE DUCK

With a sharp knife, score the skin of each duck breast with crisscross lines. Season both sides with salt and pepper.

Duck breasts with red wine sauce

Duck can be served on holiday tables instead of turkey. Crispy duck skin and a rich red wine sauce is truly a decadent meal.

BEEF POT ROAST
with winter vegetables

SERVES 6   **360 CALS PER SERVING**

Ingredients

2 tbsp sunflower oil

2½lb (1.15kg) chuck roast

4 onions, quartered

1 large rutabaga, cut into thick chunks

2 celery stalks, thickly sliced

2 large carrots, thickly sliced

¾ cup dry white wine

1 bouquet garni (page 13)

salt and black pepper

chopped parsley to garnish

1 Preheat the oven to 300°F (150°C). Heat the sunflower oil in a large Dutch oven. Add the beef and cook over high heat, turning occasionally, for about 10 minutes until browned all over.

2 Lift the beef out of the Dutch oven and put in the onions, rutabaga, celery, and carrots. Stir well to coat the vegetables in the oil, then cook, stirring occasionally, for about 5 minutes.

3 Push the vegetables to the side of the pot and place the meat in the middle, with the vegetables around it.

4 Add the wine, ¾ cup hot water, and bouquet garni, and season with salt and pepper. Bring to a boil, then cover tightly and cook in the oven for 2½–3 hours until the meat is tender.

5 Transfer the meat and vegetables to a warmed platter, cover, and keep warm.

6 Spoon the fat from the surface of the cooking liquid, then boil over high heat until the liquid is reduced by half. Taste for seasoning and strain into a warmed gravy boat. Carve the meat into thin slices, garnish with parsley, and serve with the gravy and vegetables.

BOEUF
Bourguignon

SERVES 6   490 CALS PER SERVING

Ingredients

2 tbsp sunflower oil

2lb (1kg) beef stew meat, trimmed and cut into 2in (5cm) cubes

8oz (250g) thick-cut smoked bacon, cut into strips

12 shallots

3 tbsp all-purpose flour

1¼ cups red Burgundy or any good red wine

⅔ cup beef stock

1 bouquet garni (page 13)

1 garlic clove, crushed

salt and black pepper

8oz (250g) button mushrooms

1 Preheat the oven to 325°F (170°C). Heat the oil in a large Dutch oven. Add the beef in batches and cook over high heat, turning occasionally, until browned on all sides. Remove with a slotted spoon and set aside to drain on paper towels.

2 Add the bacon and shallots and cook gently, stirring occasionally, for 3 minutes or until the bacon is crisp and the shallots are softened. Lift out and drain on paper towels.

3 Add the flour and cook, stirring, for 1 minute. Gradually blend in the wine and stock and bring to a boil, stirring until thickened.

4 Return the beef and bacon to the Dutch oven, add the bouquet garni and garlic, and season with salt and pepper. Cover and cook in the oven for 1½ hours.

5 Return the shallots to the pot, add the whole button mushrooms, and cook for 1 hour or until the beef is very tender.

6 Remove the bouquet garni and discard. Taste the sauce for seasoning before serving with warm, crusty bread.

TERIYAKI BEEF

SERVES 4   329 CALS PER SERVING

Ingredients

Marinade

½ cup dark soy sauce

⅓ cup Japanese rice wine
  or dry sherry

2 tbsp granulated sugar

For the beef

1lb (500g) flank steak,
  trimmed and cut into
  thin strips

2 tbsp sunflower oil

1 large onion, thinly sliced

1 red bell pepper, halved,
  seeded, and cut into strips

2 scallions, sliced, to garnish

1 Make the marinade: in a bowl, combine the soy sauce, rice wine
  or sherry, and sugar. Toss the steak strips in the marinade, cover,
and leave in the refrigerator overnight.

2 Remove the steak strips from the marinade, reserving the marinade.
  Heat 1 tablespoon of the oil in a wok, add the onion and red bell
pepper, and stir-fry for about 2 minutes. Remove from the wok with a
slotted spoon and set aside. Heat the remaining oil and stir-fry the
steak strips for 5 minutes or until just cooked through.

3 Return the onion and red bell pepper to the wok with the marinade
  and cook for 2 minutes or until heated through. Garnish with the
scallions before serving.

STEAK DIANE

SERVES 4   373 CALS PER SERVING

Ingredients

4 x 5–6oz (150–175g)
 flank steaks, trimmed

2 tbsp butter

2 tbsp sunflower oil

3 tbsp brandy

1 small onion, finely
 chopped

1¼ cups beef stock

2 tbsp Worcestershire sauce

1 tbsp lemon juice

1 tbsp chopped parsley

salt and black pepper

1 Place the steaks between 2 sheets of wax paper and pound
 with a rolling pin until ¼in (5mm) thick.

2 Melt the butter with the sunflower oil in a large frying pan.
 When the butter is foaming, add the pounded steaks and
cook over high heat for about 3 minutes on each side until browned.
Lift the steaks out of the frying pan and cover with foil to keep warm.

3 Pour the brandy into the pan and add the onion. Cook over
 high heat, stirring occasionally, for a few minutes until the
onion has softened and absorbed most of the brandy. Stir in
the stock, Worcestershire sauce, lemon juice, and parsley; season
with salt and pepper; and cook for about 2 minutes.

4 Return the steaks to the pan and spoon over the sauce.
 Reheat briefly, and serve hot.

FAJITAS

SERVES 4   543 CALS PER SERVING

Ingredients

Marinade

juice of 1 orange and 1 lime

3 garlic cloves, crushed

2 tbsp chopped fresh
  cilantro

a few drops of
  hot pepper sauce

salt and black pepper

Radish pico de gallo salsa

6 tomatoes, diced

10 radishes, coarsely
  chopped

5 scallions, thinly sliced

1–2 jalapeño chiles, halved,
  seeded, and chopped

¼ cup chopped fresh
  cilantro

juice of ½ lime

For the fajitas

1lb (500g) piece
  of flank steak

8 flour tortillas

chopped cilantro
  to garnish

1 avocado, pitted, peeled
  (page 45), and diced

sour cream

1 Make the marinade: in a large bowl, combine the orange and
lime juice, garlic, cilantro, and hot pepper sauce and season with salt
and pepper. Turn the steak in the marinade, cover, and marinate in the
refrigerator overnight.

2 Make the pico de gallo salsa: in a bowl, combine the tomatoes,
radishes, scallions, chiles, cilantro, lime juice, and salt to taste.
Cover and chill until ready to serve.

3 Remove the steak from the marinade and pat dry. Put the steak
under a hot broiler, 3–4in (7–10cm) from the heat, and broil for
3 minutes on each side for rare steak, 4 minutes for medium steak, or
5–6 minutes for well-done steak. Cover with foil and let stand for 5 minutes.

4 Meanwhile, warm the tortillas (see box, below).

5 Slice the steak, arrange on serving plates, and sprinkle with cilantro.
Serve with the tortillas, pico de gallo, diced avocado, and sour cream.

WARMING TORTILLAS

Sprinkle each tortilla with a little water,
and stack the tortillas in a pile.
Wrap the tortillas in foil and warm in a preheated
oven at 275°F (140°C) for 10 minutes.

BEEF
Stroganoff

SERVES 4   329 CALS PER SERVING

Ingredients

2 tbsp butter

1 tbsp sunflower oil

1½lb (750g) flank steak, trimmed and cut into strips (see box, below)

8 shallots, quartered

10oz (300g) button mushrooms, halved

salt and black pepper

1¼ cups sour cream

chopped parsley to garnish

1 Melt the butter with the oil in a large frying pan. When the butter is foaming, add the steak strips, in batches if necessary, and cook over high heat for 5 minutes or until browned all over. Remove from the pan with a slotted spoon.

2 Add the shallots and mushrooms and cook for about 5 minutes until browned.

3 Return the steak strips to the pan and season with salt and pepper. Stir in the sour cream and heat gently. Garnish with the chopped parsley, and serve at once with boiled rice.

CUTTING THE BEEF

Slice the beef at an angle into thin strips, ¼in (5mm) wide and 2in (5cm) long, using a sharp chef's knife.

HUNGARIAN
goulash

SERVES 6   474 CALS PER SERVING

Ingredients

2 tbsp sunflower oil

2lb (1kg) beef stew meat, trimmed and cut into 2in (5cm) cubes

2 large onions, sliced

1 garlic clove, crushed

1 tbsp all-purpose flour

1 tbsp paprika

2½ cups beef stock

1 x 14oz (400g) can tomatoes

2 tbsp tomato paste

salt and black pepper

2 large red bell peppers, halved, seeded, and cut into 1in (2.5cm) pieces

4 potatoes, peeled and quartered

sour cream, to serve

paprika to garnish

1 Preheat the oven to 325°F (170°C). Heat the sunflower oil in a large Dutch oven, add the beef in batches, and cook over high heat until browned.

2 Lift out the beef with a slotted spoon. Lower the heat slightly, add the onions and garlic, and cook gently, stirring occasionally, for a few minutes until soft but not colored.

3 Add the flour and paprika and cook, stirring, for 1 minute. Pour in the stock and bring to a boil, stirring.

4 Return the meat to the pot, add the tomatoes and tomato paste, and season with salt and pepper. Bring back to a boil, cover, and cook in the oven for 1 hour.

5 Add the red bell peppers and potatoes and continue cooking for 1 hour or until the potatoes and meat are tender.

6 Taste for seasoning and serve with a tablespoonful of sour cream, sprinkled with a little paprika.

THAI RED BEEF
curry

SERVES 6   327 CALS PER SERVING

Ingredients

3 tbsp sunflower oil

8 cardamom pods, split

1in (2.5cm) piece
   of cinnamon stick

6 cloves

8 black peppercorns

2lb (1kg) braising steak,
   trimmed and cut into
   1in (2.5cm) cubes

1 large onion, chopped

2in (5cm) piece of fresh
   ginger, peeled
   and grated

4 garlic cloves, crushed

4 tsp paprika

2 tsp ground cumin

1 tsp ground coriander

1 tsp salt

¼ tsp cayenne pepper or
   ½ tsp chili powder

2½ cups water

½ cup full-fat plain yogurt

1 x 14oz (400g) can
   chopped tomatoes

1 large red bell pepper,
   halved, seeded, and
   cut into chunks

2 tbsp torn fresh cilantro
   leaves, to garnish

1 Preheat the oven to 325°F (170°C). Heat the oil in a large Dutch oven; add the cardamom pods, cinnamon stick, cloves, and peppercorns; and cook over medium heat, stirring, for 1 minute. Lift out with a slotted spoon and set aside on a plate.

2 Add the beef in batches and cook over high heat until browned all over. Lift out the beef with a slotted spoon and drain on paper towels.

3 Add the onion to the pot and cook over high heat, stirring, for about 3 minutes until beginning to brown. Add the ginger, garlic, paprika, cumin, coriander, salt, cayenne or chile, and ¼ cup of the measured water. Cook, stirring, for about 1 minute.

4 Return the beef and spices to the pot, then gradually add the yogurt, stirring. Stir in the remaining water. Add the tomatoes and red bell pepper and bring to a boil. Cover and cook in the oven for 2 hours or until the beef is tender. Taste for seasoning before serving with boiled rice and garnished with the cilantro leaves.

MEAT LOAF

SERVES 6   478 CALS PER SERVING

Ingredients

1½lb (675g) ground beef

1 x 14oz (400g) can
  chopped tomatoes

¾ cup herbed
  stuffing mix

1 onion, chopped

1 carrot, coarsely shredded

3 garlic cloves, crushed

2 tbsp chopped parsley

1 large egg, beaten

1 tbsp Worcestershire sauce

salt and black pepper

4–5 slices thick-cut bacon

Special equipment

9 x 5in (23 x 12cm) loaf pan

1 Preheat the oven to 375°F (190°C). Combine the ground beef, tomatoes, stuffing mix, onion, carrot, garlic, parsley, beaten egg, and Worcestershire sauce, and season with salt and pepper.

2 Arrange bacon slices crosswise in the loaf pan, letting them hang over the sides. Put the beef mixture into the pan and fold over the bacon. Turn the loaf out into a roasting pan and bake, basting once or twice, for 1 hour.

3 Increase the heat to 450°F (230°C) and bake for 15 minutes or until the meat loaf is firm. Spoon off any fat, slice the loaf, and serve hot (or leave whole and serve cold).

LAMB CHOPS
with mint glaze

SERVES 4   304 CALS PER SERVING

Ingredients

Mint glaze

3 tbsp dry white wine

1 tbsp white wine vinegar

4 mint sprigs, leaves
   stripped and chopped

1 tbsp honey

1 tsp Dijon mustard

salt and black pepper

For the lamb

8 lamb chops,
   well trimmed

1 Make the mint glaze: combine the wine, vinegar, mint, honey, and mustard, and season with salt and pepper. Brush the glaze over the chops and marinate for about 30 minutes.

2 Place the chops on a grill or under a hot broiler, 3in (7cm) from the heat, and cook, brushing often with the glaze, for 4–6 minutes on each side, until done to your liking.

Lamb chops with mint glaze

Lamb is a versatile, delicious dish that is compatible with lots of flavors. While you can enjoy it all year long, it's stunning on a table set for a special occasion.

VARIATION

LAMB with orange glaze

Instead of the mint glaze, combine 3 tbsp orange juice with 1 tbsp each white wine vinegar, orange marmalade, and chopped fresh thyme, and 1 tsp Dijon mustard. Season with salt and pepper.

VEAL
schnitzel

SERVES 4   373 CALS PER SERVING

Ingredients

4 x 2–3oz (60–90g)
  veal cutlets

salt and black pepper

1 large egg, beaten

1 cup fresh white
  bread crumbs

4 tbsp butter

1 tbsp sunflower oil

To serve

8 anchovy fillets, drained
  and halved lengthwise

2 tbsp coarsely
  chopped capers

lemon wedges

parsley

1 Put each veal cutlet between 2 sheets of plastic wrap and pound to a ⅛in (3mm) thickness with a rolling pin. Season with salt and pepper.

2 Spread the beaten egg on a plate and sprinkle the bread crumbs on another plate. Dip each cutlet into the beaten egg, then into the bread crumbs, to coat evenly. Chill in the refrigerator for about 30 minutes.

3 Melt the butter with the oil in a large frying pan until foaming, add 2 of the cutlets, and cook for 2 minutes on each side until golden. Drain on paper towels and keep warm while cooking the remaining cutlets. Serve the veal cutlets hot, with anchovy fillets, capers, lemon wedges, and parsley.

PORK CHOPS
with stuffing

SERVES 6   345 CALS PER SERVING

Ingredients

Spinach and mushroom stuffing

1 tbsp olive oil

1 large onion, chopped

5oz (150g) cremini mushrooms, coarsely chopped

8oz (250g) baby spinach leaves, shredded

¾ cup fresh bread crumbs

salt and black pepper

For the pork chops

6 lean bone-in pork chops

olive oil for brushing

about 3oz (90g) Gruyère cheese, cut into 6 thin slices

1 Make the stuffing: heat the oil in a large frying pan, add the onion, cover, and cook gently for about 15 minutes or until soft.

2 Uncover the pan, increase the heat, and add the mushrooms. Stir-fry for 2–3 minutes, then add the spinach and stir-fry until it has just wilted. Add the bread crumbs, season with salt and pepper, and stir well. Let cool.

3 Brush the chops on each side with oil and season well. Put under a hot broiler, 4in (10cm) from the heat, and broil for 7–8 minutes on each side or until cooked through and golden brown.

4 Spoon 1 tablespoon of the stuffing mixture on top of each chop and top with a slice of cheese. Broil for 3–4 minutes until the cheese has melted.

5 Meanwhile, heat a little oil in a small nonstick frying pan. Put the remaining stuffing into the pan, then press down and level with a wooden spoon so that the stuffing forms a thick pancake.

6 Cook the stuffing for about 5 minutes until the underside is brown and crisp. Transfer the pan to the broiler for 2–3 minutes to brown the top. Turn upside down onto a plate and slice into 6 wedges. Serve a wedge of stuffing with each chop.

PORK TENDERLOIN
with chile and coconut

SERVES 6   332 CALS PER SERVING

Ingredients

Spice mix

1in (2.5cm) piece of fresh ginger, peeled and grated

2 fresh red chiles, halved, seeded, and finely chopped

1 garlic clove, crushed

1 tbsp mild curry powder

salt and black pepper

For the pork

1½lb (675g) pork fillet (tenderloin), trimmed and cut into ¼in (5mm) strips

2 tbsp sunflower oil

8 scallions, cut into 1in (2.5cm) pieces

1 large red bell pepper, halved, seeded, and cut into thin strips

1 x 14oz (400g) can chopped tomatoes

1 x 14oz (400g) can coconut milk

2 tbsp chopped fresh cilantro

1 tbsp lemon juice

cilantro sprigs to garnish

1 Make the spice mix: in a bowl, combine the ginger, chiles, garlic, and curry powder and season with salt and pepper. Turn the pork in the mix, cover, and marinate in the refrigerator for 2 hours.

2 Heat a wok or large frying pan, add the oil, and heat until hot. Add the strips of pork in batches and stir-fry over high heat for 5 minutes or until browned all over.

3 Add the scallions and stir-fry for 1 minute. Add the red bell pepper and stir-fry for 1 minute, then add the tomatoes, coconut, and ¼ cup water. Bring to a boil, cover, and simmer very gently for 15 minutes or until the pork is tender.

4 Add the chopped cilantro, lemon juice, and salt and pepper to taste. Garnish with cilantro sprigs before serving with rice.

DICING FRESH CHILES

Cut the chile in half lengthwise. Remove the stalk and core and scrape out the fleshy white ribs and seeds.

Set the cut side up and cut into thin strips. Hold the strips together and cut across to make cubes.

PORK CHOPS
with mixed peppercorns

SERVES 4   567 CALS PER SERVING

Ingredients

4 lean boneless pork chops

salt

3–4 tbsp mixed or
   black peppercorns

2 tbsp butter

1½ cups dry white wine

1½ cups chicken stock

¾ cup heavy cream

1 Season the chops on each side with salt. Coarsely crush the peppercorns, spread them on a plate, and press the chops into them to encrust the surface of the meat. Turn the chops over and repeat on the other side. Cover and set aside for about 30 minutes, if you have the time.

2 Melt the butter in a large frying pan, add the pork chops, and cook over medium heat for 5 minutes on each side or until the meat is just cooked through but still juicy. Lift the chops out and keep hot.

3 Pour the wine into the pan and boil until it has reduced by half, stirring to mix in the peppercorns and the sediment from the bottom of the pan.

4 Pour in the stock and cook for 5 minutes. Strain the sauce to remove the peppercorns, then return to the pan and boil for 3 minutes or until the sauce is reduced but not too thick.

5 Add the cream and cook, stirring, over high heat until the sauce is reduced and thickened. Return the pork chops to the pan, heat through, and serve at once with a little of the sauce poured over them, accompanied by potato wedges and grilled mushrooms.

SWEET AND SOUR
Chinese spareribs

SERVES 4   491 CALS PER SERVING

Ingredients

2½lb (1.25kg) pork spareribs

salt and black pepper

scallions to garnish (optional)

Sweet and sour sauce

1in (2.5cm) piece of fresh
  ginger, peeled and grated

2 garlic cloves, crushed

2 tbsp soy sauce

2 tbsp rice wine or dry sherry

2 tbsp hoisin sauce

2 tbsp tomato paste

1 tbsp sesame oil (optional)

1 tbsp granulated sugar

1 Preheat the oven to 275°F (140°C). Lay the ribs in 1 layer in a roasting pan, season with salt and pepper, and cook for 1½ hours.

2 Make the sauce: combine all the ingredients in a small pan and heat gently.

3 Spoon the sauce over the ribs, turning them to coat. Increase the oven temperature to 350°F (180°C) and cook for 25–30 minutes. Serve hot, garnished with scallions if you like.

VARIATION
SPICED
spareribs

Add 1 tbsp brown sugar,
½ tsp grated nutmeg,
and ¼ tsp each ground
cloves and ground
cinnamon to the sauce.

SHRIMP TACOS

SERVES 4   414 CALS PER SERVING

Ingredients

2 tbsp sunflower oil

2 onions, chopped

3 garlic cloves, crushed

1 green bell pepper, halved, seeded, and diced

1 tbsp paprika

2 tsp mild chili powder

½ tsp ground cumin

4 ripe firm tomatoes, chopped

1lb (500g) cooked peeled shrimp

2 tbsp chopped fresh cilantro

salt and black pepper

12 taco shells

1 round head lettuce, shredded

sliced pickled jalapeño chiles, large cooked peeled shrimp, and cilantro leaves to garnish

1 Preheat the oven to 350°F (180°C). Heat the oil in a large frying pan, add the onions, and cook gently, stirring occasionally, for 3–5 minutes until softened but not colored. Add the garlic and diced green bell pepper and cook, stirring occasionally, for 3 minutes or until the pepper is soft.

2 Stir in the paprika, chili powder, and cumin, and cook, stirring, for 1 minute. Add the tomatoes and cook for 3–5 minutes until soft.

3 Lower the heat, stir in the shrimp and chopped cilantro, and season with salt and pepper.

4 Meanwhile, heat the taco shells in the oven for 3 minutes or according to package instructions.

5 Spoon the shrimp mixture into the taco shells, top with the shredded lettuce, and garnish with chiles, shrimp, and cilantro. Serve at once.

JUMBO SHRIMP
with tarragon sauce

SERVES 4   252 CALS PER SERVING

Ingredients

Tarragon sauce

⅔ cup sour cream

¼ cup chopped
  fresh tarragon

1 tsp Dijon mustard

squeeze of lemon juice

salt and black pepper

For the shrimp

12 uncooked jumbo shrimp
  in their shells

olive oil for brushing

1¼ cups dry white wine

1 garlic clove, crushed

4 tbsp chopped fresh parsley

lemon and tarragon
  to garnish

1 Make the tarragon sauce: combine the sour cream, tarragon, mustard, and lemon juice, and season with salt and pepper.

2 Heat a heavy frying pan. Brush the shrimp with oil, add to the pan, and cook the shrimp over high heat for 2 minutes or until pink.

3 Keeping the heat high, add ⅔ cup of the wine and the garlic. Boil rapidly for 2–3 minutes, then stir in 2 tablespoons of the parsley.

4 When the wine has reduced slightly, lower the heat, add the remaining wine, and season with salt and pepper. Simmer for 5 minutes or until the shrimp have released their juices into the wine.

5 Spoon the cooking juices over the shrimp, sprinkle with the remaining parsley, and garnish with lemon and sprigs of fresh tarragon. Serve hot, with the tarragon sauce.

SCALLOPS
with spicy cashew sauce

SERVES 6   276 CALS PER SERVING

Ingredients

⅔ cup toasted, salted cashews

3 tbsp sunflower oil

3 garlic cloves, crushed

1lb (500g) scallops

1 onion, chopped

1 green bell pepper, halved, seeded, and cut into thin strips

1 fresh red chile, halved, seeded, and finely chopped

½ tsp turmeric

1 cup fish stock

1 tsp coarse-grain mustard

salt and black pepper

1 Grind the cashews in a food processor or nut grinder until smooth.

2 Heat the oil in a large frying pan, add the garlic and scallops, and stir-fry for 2 minutes or just until the scallops turn opaque. Remove with a slotted spoon.

3 Add the onion, green bell pepper, and chile to the frying pan and cook gently, stirring occasionally, for 3–5 minutes until the onion is soft but not colored. Add the turmeric and cook, stirring, for 1 minute.

4 Add the ground cashews and stock to the mixture in the frying pan, bring to a boil, and simmer for 5–10 minutes until the sauce thickens.

5 Stir the scallops into the sauce, add the mustard and salt and pepper to taste, and gently warm through. Serve hot.

Cook's know-how

If you are short on time, use 2 heaping tablespoons of cashew nut butter or peanut butter (smooth or crunchy) instead of grinding the cashews in step 1.

MUSSEL GRATIN

SERVES 4   448 CALS PER SERVING

Ingredients

¾ cup dry white wine

1 shallot, finely chopped

1 garlic clove, crushed

6lb (3kg) large mussels, cleaned (page 15)

1¼ cups half-and-half

3 tbsp chopped parsley

salt and black pepper

¾ cup fresh white bread crumbs

2 tbsp butter, melted

1 Pour the wine into a large saucepan, add the chopped shallot and crushed garlic, and bring to a boil. Simmer for 2 minutes.

2 Add the mussels, cover tightly, and return to a boil. Cook, shaking the pan frequently, for 5–6 minutes until the mussels open.

3 Using a slotted spoon, transfer the mussels to a large bowl. Discard any that have not opened; do not try to force them open.

4 Strain the cooking liquid into a saucepan, bring to a boil, and simmer until reduced to about 3 tablespoons. Add the half-and-half and heat through. Stir in half of the parsley and season with salt and pepper.

5 Remove the top shell of each mussel and discard. Arrange the mussels, in their bottom shells, on a large ovenproof serving dish.

6 Spoon the sauce over the mussels and sprinkle with the bread crumbs and melted butter. Cook under a hot broiler, 4in (10cm) from the heat, for 3–5 minutes until golden. Garnish with the remaining parsley and serve at once.

Cook's know-how

Mussels are often sold by volume: 1½ pints (900ml) is equivalent to 1½lb (675g), which will yield about 12oz (350g) shelled mussels.

SPICY CLAMS
with cilantro pesto

SERVES 4–6   233–349 CALS PER SERVING

Ingredients

Cilantro pesto

12 cilantro sprigs

2 tbsp olive oil

1 large garlic clove, coarsely chopped

1 fresh jalapeño chile, halved, seeded, and coarsely chopped

salt and black pepper

For the spicy clams

¼ cup olive oil

6 ripe firm tomatoes, diced

4 garlic cloves, crushed

1 tbsp mild chili powder

about 4 dozen baby clams, cleaned (page 15)

2½ cups fish stock, or 1¼ cups each dry white wine and fish stock

juice of ½ lime

1 lime cut into wedges

1 Make the cilantro pesto: strip the cilantro leaves from the stalks. Purée the cilantro leaves, olive oil, garlic, and jalapeño chile in a food processor or blender until smooth. Season with salt and pepper, and set aside.

2 Heat the oil in a large saucepan; add the tomatoes, garlic, and chili powder; and cook gently, stirring occasionally, for 8 minutes or until slightly thickened.

3 Add the clams and stir for about 1 minute, then pour in the stock. Cover the pan tightly and cook the clams over medium heat, shaking the pan frequently, for about 5–8 minutes until the clams open. Discard any that have not opened; do not try to force them open.

4 Using a slotted spoon, transfer the clams to a warmed bowl.

5 Pour the cooking juices into a small pan and boil until reduced by about half. Add the lime juice and season to taste, then pour the sauce over the clams.

6 Serve the clams immediately, with lime wedges and cilantro pesto.

BROILED TROUT
with cucumber and dill

SERVES 4 . 435 CALS PER SERVING

Ingredients

1 cucumber, peeled

2 tbsp butter

small bunch of fresh
  dill, chopped

salt and black pepper

juice of 1 lemon

4 x 12–14oz (350–400g)
  trout, cleaned (page 14)

dill sprigs to garnish

dill cream sauce (see box,
  below) to serve

1 Cut the cucumber in half lengthwise and scoop out the seeds, then cut the flesh across into ¼in (5mm) slices. Melt the butter in a saucepan, add the cucumber, and cook gently for 2 minutes.

2 In a bowl, combine two-thirds of the cooked cucumber with the chopped dill, season with salt and pepper, and sprinkle with the lemon juice. Stuff the trout with the mixture.

3 Line a broiler pan with foil. Arrange the trout on the foil and put the remaining cucumber around them.

4 Broil the trout under a hot broiler, 4in (10cm) from the heat, for 4–7 minutes on each side until the flesh flakes easily.

5 Garnish the trout with dill sprigs and serve at once with buttered new potatoes and the dill cream sauce on the side.

DILL CREAM SAUCE

Purée 1¼ cups half-and-half, 6 tbsp butter, 1 large egg yolk, the juice of 1 lemon, and 1 tsp all-purpose flour in a food processor until smooth. Transfer the mixture to a small saucepan and heat very gently, stirring constantly, until the sauce has thickened and will coat the back of a spoon. Add salt and pepper to taste, then stir in 2 tbsp chopped fresh dill and 1 tbsp snipped fresh chives.

TUNA WITH FENNEL
and tomato relish

SERVES 4   467 CALS PER SERVING

Ingredients

¼ cup olive oil

juice of ½ lemon

3 garlic cloves, crushed

4 x 6oz (175g) tuna steaks, about 1in (2.5cm) thick

salt and black pepper

lime wedges and fennel tops to garnish

Fennel and tomato relish

1 small fennel bulb, chopped

2 ripe but firm tomatoes, finely chopped

2 tbsp olive oil

1 tbsp lemon juice

1 tbsp tapenade (see box, below)

1 garlic clove, chopped

1 Combine the olive oil, lemon juice, and garlic in a large nonmetallic dish. Add the tuna steaks and turn to coat. Cover the dish and marinate in the refrigerator, turning occasionally, for about 1 hour.

2 Meanwhile, make the relish: put the fennel, tomatoes, olive oil, lemon juice, tapenade, and garlic into a bowl and stir well to combine.

3 Remove the tuna from the marinade, reserving the marinade. Cook the tuna under a hot broiler, 3in (7cm) from the heat, basting once or twice with the reserved marinade, for 3–4 minutes on each side.

4 Season the tuna with salt and pepper and top with the fennel and tomato relish. Garnish with lime wedges and fennel tops before serving with a simple green salad.

Cook's know-how

Tapenade comes from Provence in the south of France. It is a tangy paste made of typical Provençal ingredients—black olives, anchovies, capers, and fruity olive oil. It is sold in tubes, jars, and tubs at supermarkets.

TUNA STEAKS
with orange relish

SERVES 4   429 CALS PER SERVING

Ingredients

Marinade

3 tbsp olive oil

juice of 1 orange

juice of 1 lemon

3 garlic cloves, crushed

salt and black pepper

4 x 6oz (175g) tuna steaks

For the orange relish

2 oranges, peeled,
   separated into
   segments, and diced

3 tbsp olive oil

2 tbsp chopped
   fresh cilantro

1 Make the marinade: in a shallow nonmetallic dish, combine the olive oil, orange and lemon juices, and garlic and season with salt and pepper. Turn the tuna steaks in the marinade, cover, and marinate in the refrigerator for about 1 hour.

2 Make the orange relish: in a bowl, combine the oranges, olive oil, and cilantro and season with salt and pepper to taste.

3 Remove the tuna from the marinade, reserving the marinade. Place the steaks under a hot broiler, 3in (7cm) from the heat, and broil, basting once or twice with the marinade, for 3 minutes on each side (or cooked to your liking), or until the flesh is opaque and flakes easily. Serve hot, with the relish.

Cook's know-how

When marinating fish, leave it for no more than 4 hours. After this time the acid in the marinade will start to seep deep into the fish, which will make it dry when it is cooked.

HERB ROASTED
salmon

SERVES 4   396 CALS PER SERVING

Ingredients

4 x 5oz (150g) salmon
  tail fillets, skinned

salt and black pepper

a little vegetable oil

4oz (125g) low-fat garlic-
  and-herb cream cheese

lemon wedges, to garnish

flat-leaf parsley sprigs,
  to garnish

Topping

¾ cup fresh white
  bread crumbs

1oz (30g) aged Cheddar
  cheese, grated

2 tbsp chopped fresh
  flat-leaf parsley

finely grated zest of 1 lime

1   Preheat the oven to 425°F (220°C). Season the salmon on both sides
    with salt and pepper. Place on lightly oiled foil on a baking sheet and
spread with the cream cheese, not going quite to the edges.

2   Mix the topping ingredients together, adding seasoning to taste,
    then sprinkle over the salmon. (You can prepare ahead to this stage,
cover the salmon, and keep it in the refrigerator for up to 12 hours.)

3   Cook in the oven for 15 minutes or until the salmon is opaque
    and the flesh flakes easily. Garnish with lemon and parsley.

MUSHROOM-STUFFED
sole fillets

SERVES 4   568 CALS PER SERVING

Ingredients

4 tbsp butter

1 onion, finely chopped

12oz (350g) mushrooms, finely chopped

2 large lemon sole, each cut into 4 fillets and skinned (page 15)

1 cup dry white wine

2 tsp chopped fresh tarragon

salt and black pepper

1 cup heavy cream

squeeze of lemon juice

fresh tarragon sprigs to garnish

1 Preheat the oven to 350°F (180°C). Melt half of the butter in a saucepan, add the onion and mushrooms, and cook gently for 5 minutes.

2 Roll the fillets (see box, below), with the skinned sides facing inward. Stand them in a shallow baking dish and fill with the mushrooms and onion.

3 Add the wine, tarragon, and salt and pepper to taste. Cover and bake for 15 minutes or until the fish is opaque and flakes easily.

4 Remove the fish from the dish and keep warm. Pour the juices into a saucepan and boil for 3 minutes or until reduced by half. Stir in the cream and lemon juice, heat through gently, and taste for seasoning before serving, garnished with sprigs of fresh tarragon.

ROLLING THE FILLETS

Bring around the 2 ends of each fillet to form a circle, with the smaller tail end on the outside. **Thread** a wooden toothpick through both ends of each fillet to secure.

Best-ever fried fish

Here is my version
of the famous fish 'n' chips:
a quintessential British dish that
is universally loved and a must
when visiting the ocean!

BEST-EVER FRIED FISH

SERVES 4   298 CALS PER SERVING

Ingredients

3 tbsp all-purpose flour

salt and black pepper

1 large egg, beaten

¾ cup fresh white
   bread crumbs

4 large sole fillets, skinned

2 tbsp sunflower oil

lemon wedges to garnish

1 Sprinkle the flour into a shallow dish and season with salt and
pepper. Pour the beaten egg into another dish and sprinkle the
bread crumbs into a third.

2 Lightly coat the fish fillets with bread crumbs (see box, below).

3 Heat the oil in a large frying pan, add the coated fillets, in 2 batches
if necessary, and fry over high heat for 2–3 minutes on each side
until they are crisp, golden, and juicy inside.

4 Lift the fillets out of the frying pan with a fish spatula and then
let drain briefly on paper towels. Serve the fish at once, garnished
with the lemon wedges and accompanied by green peas and steak fries
(page 201).

COATING A FISH FILLET

Dip the fillet into the seasoned flour to coat. Shake off any excess.

Dip the floured fillet into the beaten egg, letting any excess drain off.

Dip the fillet into the bread crumbs, making sure it is evenly coated.

CAJUN-SPICED
red snapper

SERVES 4   258 CALS PER SERVING

Ingredients

Cajun spice mixture

3 tbsp all-purpose flour

1 garlic clove, crushed

1 tbsp paprika

1 tsp ground cumin

1 tsp hot chili powder

For the fish

4 x 5–6oz (150–175g) red
   snapper fillets

2 tbsp butter

greens to serve

For the cilantro butter

9 tbsp butter

2 tbsp chopped
   fresh cilantro

1 tbsp lemon juice

1 tsp ground coriander

salt and black pepper

1 Make the Cajun spice mixture: combine the flour, garlic, paprika, cumin, and chili powder.

2 Rub over the red snapper fillets, cover, and marinate in the refrigerator for about 30 minutes.

3 Melt the 2 tablespoons of butter in a large frying pan, add the fillets, and cook gently for 2–3 minutes on each side until the fish is opaque and the flesh flakes easily.

4 Make the cilantro butter: soften the butter and blend in the chopped fresh cilantro, lemon juice, and ground coriander, and season with salt and black pepper. Chill.

5 Top the fillets with pats of cilantro butter, garnish with greens, and serve hot with rice.

Cook's know-how

You can buy premixed Cajun seasoning, but it tends to include dried garlic and onion salt, both of which overpower the spices in the mix. This simple version uses chili powder, which is not just ground dried chiles as its name suggests, but a special fiery mixture of chile with herbs and spices. Check the label before buying.

SEA BASS
with lemon butter sauce

SERVES 4   363 CALS PER SERVING

Ingredients

sunflower oil for greasing

2¼lb (1.1kg) sea bass, cleaned and filleted (pages 14–15)

4 tarragon sprigs

1 lemon, sliced

salt and black pepper

2 tbsp dry white wine

Lemon butter sauce

¾ cup half-and-half

juice of ½ lemon

3 tbsp butter, melted

1 large egg yolk

1 tsp all-purpose flour

white pepper

1 tsp chopped fresh tarragon

1 Preheat the oven to 400°F (200°C). Put a large piece of foil onto a baking sheet and brush lightly with oil. Place the sea bass onto the foil, tuck 3 of the tarragon sprigs and all but 1–2 of the lemon slices inside the cavity, and sprinkle with salt and black pepper.

2 Season the outside of the fish and lift up the sides of the foil. Pour the wine over the fish, then seal the foil into a loose package. Bake in the oven for 30 minutes or until the flesh is opaque and flakes easily.

3 Meanwhile, make the sauce: whisk the half-and-half in a pan with the lemon juice, butter, egg yolk, and flour until mixed. Heat very gently, stirring constantly, until the mixture is thick enough to coat the back of a spoon. Season with salt and white pepper and stir in the tarragon. Keep warm.

4 Remove the sea bass from the foil and arrange on a warmed serving dish. Pour over the cooking juices. Garnish with the remaining lemon slices and tarragon sprig, and serve at once. Serve the warm lemon butter sauce separately.

PAD THAI
with shrimp

SERVES 6   245 CALS PER SERVING

Ingredients

8oz (250g) wide
   rice noodles

2 tbsp olive oil

2 skinless, boneless chicken
   breasts (about 4oz/125g
   each), cut into thin strips

1 small fresh red chile,
   halved, seeded,
   and finely chopped

1in (2.5cm) piece of
   fresh ginger, peeled
   and finely grated

1in (2.5cm) piece of fresh
   lemongrass from the
   lower part of the stalk,
   very finely chopped

4oz (125g) peeled
   raw jumbo shrimp

3oz (90g) oyster
   mushrooms, thinly sliced

4oz (125g) sugar snap
   peas, trimmed and
   sliced on the diagonal

3 tbsp soy sauce

2 tbsp lime juice

1 tbsp fish sauce

salt and black pepper

¼ cup salted or unsalted
   peanuts, to serve

a handful of fresh cilantro,
   chopped to serve

1 Cook the noodles according to package instructions. Drain, refresh under cold running water, and set aside.

2 Heat 1 tablespoon of the oil in a wok or large nonstick frying pan and stir-fry the chicken over high heat for 2 minutes or until golden brown and cooked through. Remove with a slotted spoon and set aside.

3 Heat the remaining oil in the pan; add the chile, ginger, lemongrass, shrimp, mushrooms, and peas; and stir-fry for 1 minute. Add the soy sauce, lime juice, and fish sauce and season with salt and pepper. Return the chicken to the pan and add the noodles. Stir-fry until the shrimp is pink and everything is piping hot, for 2–3 minutes. Serve hot, with peanuts and cilantro scattered on top.

SHRIMP
tagliatelle

SERVES 4   294 CALS PER SERVING

Ingredients

2 tbsp olive oil

1 large onion, chopped

1 garlic clove, crushed

12oz (350g) button
  mushrooms, halved

1lb (500g) tomatoes,
  chopped into small
  pieces, cores removed

salt and black pepper

1lb (500g) tagliatelle

12oz (375g) cooked
  peeled shrimp

½ cup full-fat crème fraîche

¼ cup chopped parsley
  to garnish

1 Heat the oil in a large pan, add the onion and garlic, and cook gently, stirring, for 3–5 minutes until softened but not colored. Add the mushrooms and cook over high heat, stirring, for about 5 minutes.

2 Add the tomatoes, season with salt and pepper, and simmer gently, uncovered, for about 20 minutes or until the mixture has thickened.

3 Meanwhile, cook the tagliatelle in a large saucepan of boiling salted water for 8–10 minutes until just tender.

4 Add the shrimp and crème fraîche to the tomato mixture and cook gently for about 2 minutes until the shrimp is heated through. Taste for seasoning.

5 Drain the tagliatelle thoroughly and pile onto warmed serving plates. Spoon the shrimp mixture on top, sprinkle with parsley, and serve at once.

VARIATION

PASTA with smoked salmon and shrimp

Substitute 4oz (125g) smoked salmon, cut into bite-sized pieces, for 4oz (125g) of the shrimp. Add the smoked salmon after the shrimp have been heated through in step 4.

PASTA SHELLS
with scallops

SERVES 4   753 CALS PER SERVING

Ingredients

8 large scallops, each
  cut into 3 slices

juice of 1 lemon

1 slice of onion

6 black peppercorns

1 small bay leaf

1lb (500g) pasta shells

3 tsp butter

chopped parsley and
  lemon slices to garnish

Sauce

3 tbsp butter

4oz (125g) button
  mushrooms, sliced

3 tbsp all-purpose flour

¾ cup heavy cream or
  full-fat crème fraîche

1 tbsp tomato paste

salt and black pepper

1 Put the scallops into a pan with ⅓ cup water, half the lemon juice, and the onion, peppercorns, and bay leaf.

2 Bring to a gentle simmer, cover, and poach very gently for 2–3 minutes or until the scallops are opaque.

3 Remove the scallops with a slotted spoon, strain the liquid, and reserve.

4 Make the sauce: melt the butter in a saucepan, add the mushrooms, and cook gently, stirring occasionally, for 2 minutes. Sprinkle in the flour and cook, stirring, for 1 minute. Remove from the heat and blend in the strained poaching liquid. Cook, stirring, for 1 minute until thickened.

5 Add the cream and tomato paste and bring to a boil, stirring constantly until the mixture thickens. Simmer for 2 minutes, then add salt and pepper to taste.

6 Cook the pasta shells in a large saucepan of boiling salted water for 8–10 minutes or until tender. Drain, then toss with the butter and the remaining lemon juice. Add the scallops to the sauce and heat through very gently.

7 Pile the pasta on warmed serving plates and spoon the sauce on top. Serve at once, garnished with the parsley and lemon slices.

Penne with spinach and Stilton

Originating from the north of England, Stilton is licensed to be made in only 6 dairies situated in 3 counties. You can substitute any blue cheese for the Stilton if you're having trouble finding it.

PENNE
with spinach and Stilton

SERVES 6   976 CALS PER SERVING

Ingredients

1lb (500g) penne

salt and black pepper

3 tbsp butter

2 large garlic cloves, crushed

8oz (250g) cremini
  mushrooms, sliced

1¼ cups heavy cream

1 large egg, lightly
  beaten (optional)

3oz (90g) spinach leaves,
  coarsely shredded

3oz (90g) blue Stilton
  cheese, coarsely grated

juice of ½ lemon

pinch of grated nutmeg

1 Cook the pasta in boiling salted water for 8–10 minutes until just tender.

2 Meanwhile, melt the butter in a large pan, add the garlic, and cook, stirring, for 1 minute. Add the mushrooms and cook, stirring occasionally, for 2 minutes. Stir in the cream and boil for 2–3 minutes until the mixture reaches a coating consistency.

3 Drain the pasta, add to the mushroom and cream mixture with the egg (if using), stir well, and heat through. Add the spinach, Stilton cheese, lemon juice, nutmeg, and pepper to taste, and stir well to coat the pasta. Serve immediately.

FETTUCCINE
primavera

SERVES 6   554 CALS PER SERVING

Ingredients

4oz (125g) asparagus, trimmed and cut into bite-sized pieces

4oz (125g) broccoli florets

1 zucchini, sliced

salt and black pepper

3 tbsp olive oil

½ red and ½ yellow bell pepper, halved, seeded, and diced

3 garlic cloves, crushed

1 x 7oz (200g) can chopped tomatoes

3oz (90g) frozen peas

½ cup heavy cream

1lb (500g) fettuccine

¼ cup shredded fresh basil

3oz (90g) Parmesan cheese, grated, to serve

1 Cook the asparagus, broccoli, and zucchini in boiling salted water for 3 minutes or until just tender. Drain, rinse under cold running water, and set aside.

2 Heat the oil in a large, deep frying pan, add the peppers and garlic, and cook, stirring, for 4 minutes or until the peppers are softened.

3 Add the tomatoes and the peas and cook for 5 minutes or until the liquid in the pan is reduced by half.

4 Add the asparagus, broccoli, and zucchini; stir in the cream; and boil for 1–2 minutes to reduce the liquid and concentrate the flavor. Add salt and pepper to taste and remove from the heat.

5 Cook the fettuccine in a large saucepan of boiling salted water for 8–10 minutes until just tender.

6 Drain the fettuccine thoroughly, add to the sauce, and toss over high heat. Stir in the shredded basil and serve at once, sprinkled with Parmesan cheese.

TUNA AND FENNEL
pasta bake

SERVES 6   512 CALS PER SERVING

Ingredients

8oz (250g) pasta shells
  (conchiglie)

salt and black pepper

1 tbsp sunflower oil

1 fennel bulb, trimmed
  and finely sliced

1 onion, finely sliced

4 tbsp butter

½ cup all-purpose flour

2½ cups milk

1 x 7oz (200g) can tuna in
  oil, drained and flaked

3 hard-boiled eggs,
  coarsely chopped

4oz (125g) aged Cheddar
  cheese, grated

2 tbsp chopped parsley
  to garnish

1 Preheat the oven to 400°F (200°C). Cook the pasta shells in boiling salted water for 8–10 minutes until just tender. Drain thoroughly and set aside.

2 Heat the sunflower oil in a large frying pan, add the fennel and onion, and cook for 3–5 minutes until softened but not browned. Set aside.

3 Melt the butter in a large saucepan, sprinkle in the flour, and cook, stirring, for 1 minute. Remove from the heat and gradually blend in the milk. Bring to a boil, stirring until the mixture thickens. Simmer for 2–3 minutes.

4 Stir in the pasta, fennel, onion, tuna, eggs, and cheese. Season with salt and pepper, then turn the mixture into a shallow ovenproof dish.

5 Bake in the oven for about 30 minutes or until heated through and golden brown on top. Serve hot, sprinkled with chopped parsley.

SPAGHETTI
alla carbonara

SERVES 4   906 CALS PER SERVING

Ingredients

1lb (500g) spaghetti

salt and black pepper

6oz (175g) diced pancetta
   or thick-cut bacon

1 garlic clove, crushed

4 large eggs

4oz (125g) Parmesan
   cheese, grated

¾ cup half-and-half

chopped parsley to garnish

1 Cook the spaghetti in a large saucepan of boiling salted water for 8–10 minutes until just tender.

2 Meanwhile, put the pancetta or bacon into a frying pan and heat gently for 7 minutes until the fat runs. Increase the heat and add the garlic. Cook for 2–3 minutes or until the bacon is crisp.

3 Break the eggs into a bowl. Add the bacon and garlic mixture, using a slotted spoon. Add the Parmesan cheese, season generously with salt and pepper, and whisk until well blended.

4 Drain the spaghetti and return to the hot pan. Stir in the bacon and egg mixture and toss quickly until the egg just begins to set. Stir in the half-and-half and heat gently. Serve at once, sprinkled with parsley.

VARIATION

SPAGHETTI
alfredo

Heat ¾ cup heavy cream with 2 tbsp butter until the mixture has thickened. Set aside. Cook the pasta, drain, then add to the cream mixture. Add ½ cup more cream, 3oz (90g) Parmesan cheese, and a pinch of grated nutmeg, and season with salt and pepper. Heat gently until thickened, and serve.

Cook's know-how

It is best to buy a whole piece of Parmesan cheese and grate the quantity you need for a given dish. Pregrated Parmesan is less economical and lacks the flavor of freshly grated Parmesan.

RICOTTA
and spinach ravioli

SERVES 3   341 CALS PER SERVING

Ingredients

Basic pasta dough

1¾ cups bread flour

3 large eggs

1 tsp salt

1 tbsp olive oil

Filling

4oz (125g) ricotta cheese

2oz (60g) Parmesan
  cheese, grated

1 large egg, beaten

¼ tsp grated nutmeg

8oz (250g) spinach leaves,
  cooked, squeezed dry,
  and chopped

salt and black pepper

2 tbsp butter to serve

1   Sift the flour into a mound on a work surface. Make a well in the middle and add the eggs, salt, and oil. Using your fingertips, gradually draw the flour into the egg mixture until a sticky ball of dough is formed.

2   Knead the dough on a floured work surface for 10 minutes or until the pasta dough is smooth and no longer sticks to the work surface.

3   Shape the dough into a ball, put into an oiled plastic bag, and let rest at room temperature for about 30 minutes. Roll out the dough very thinly on a lightly floured work surface into a 15in (37cm) square. Leave the pasta uncovered for about 20 minutes to dry out slightly.

4   Make the filling: beat together the ricotta, half of the Parmesan, the egg, nutmeg, and spinach. Season with salt and pepper.

5   Fill, cook, and drain the ravioli (see box, below). Serve with butter, the remaining Parmesan, and black pepper.

FILLING AND COOKING THE RAVIOLI

Place 18 spoonfuls of filling at regular intervals onto one half of the pasta. Lightly brush the pasta between the filling with water. Roll the remaining pasta around a rolling pin and unroll over the filling. Press the pasta around the edges and the spoonfuls of filling.

With a knife, pastry wheel, or pastry cutter, cut into round or square ravioli. Leave for about 30 minutes, turning once, until dried out. Add a little oil to a large saucepan of boiling salted water, add the ravioli, and cook for 4–5 minutes until just tender. Drain and serve immediately.

PASTA SPIRALS
with herbed meatballs

SERVES 8   384 CALS PER SERVING

Ingredients

Tomato-basil sauce

1 tbsp olive oil

1 onion, coarsely chopped

2 garlic cloves, crushed

2 x 14oz (400g) cans
chopped tomatoes

1 tsp granulated sugar

salt and black pepper

1 tbsp chopped fresh basil

For the meatballs

1lb (500g) ground turkey
or chicken

2 tbsp chopped parsley

1 tsp chopped fresh thyme

2oz (60g) Parmesan
cheese, grated

½ cup fresh bread crumbs

1 large egg, beaten

a little olive oil, for frying

For the pasta

1lb (500g) pasta
spirals (rotini)

shredded fresh basil
to garnish

a little Parmesan cheese
to garnish, grated

1 Make the tomato-basil sauce: heat the oil in a deep frying pan, add the onion and garlic, and cook gently, stirring occasionally, for 3–4 minutes.

2 Add the tomatoes and sugar, season with salt and pepper, and stir well. Simmer, uncovered, for about 20 minutes, stirring occasionally, until the onion is soft and the sauce reduced.

3 Make the meatballs: in a large bowl, combine the ground turkey or chicken, parsley, thyme, Parmesan cheese, bread crumbs, and egg, then season with salt and pepper. With dampened hands, shape the mixture into balls about the size of large walnuts.

4 Heat a little oil in a large frying pan, add the meatballs, and cook for about 8 minutes until browned and cooked through. Lift out with a slotted spoon and drain on paper towels. Add to the tomato sauce and heat gently for about 5 minutes.

5 Meanwhile, cook the pasta in a large pan of boiling salted water for 8–10 minutes until tender. Drain thoroughly and top with the meatballs and sauce. Serve, garnished with shredded basil and grated Parmesan.

CANNELLONI
with ricotta and spinach

SERVES 6   462 CALS PER SERVING

Ingredients

Tomato sauce

1 tbsp olive oil

2 celery stalks, chopped

1 small onion, chopped

1 carrot, chopped

1 garlic clove, crushed

1¼ cups chicken stock

2 x 14oz (400g) cans
  chopped tomatoes

2 tbsp tomato paste

salt and black pepper

2oz (60g) sun-dried
  tomatoes in oil,
  drained and chopped

For the filling

2 tbsp olive oil

1 small onion, chopped

1 garlic clove, crushed

1lb (500g) spinach, chopped

1lb (500g) ricotta cheese

¼ tsp grated nutmeg

For the cannelloni

butter for greasing

18 cannelloni tubes

1oz (30g) Parmesan
  cheese, grated

1 Preheat the oven to 400°F (200°C). Make the tomato sauce: heat the oil in a saucepan; add the celery, onion, carrot, and garlic; and cook gently for 3–5 minutes until softened. Stir in the stock, tomatoes, and tomato paste, season with salt and pepper, and bring to a boil. Cover and simmer, stirring occasionally, for 30 minutes.

2 Meanwhile, make the filling: heat the oil in a large pan, add the onion and garlic, and cook for 3–5 minutes until softened. Add the spinach and cook over high heat for 1–2 minutes. Cool slightly, add the ricotta and nutmeg, and season with salt and pepper.

3 Purée the tomato sauce in a food processor, then stir in the chopped sun-dried tomatoes.

4 Grease an ovenproof dish. Spoon the spinach filling into the cannelloni. Arrange in the dish, cover with the sauce, and sprinkle with Parmesan. Bake for 30 minutes. Serve hot, with a little extra Parmesan cheese grated over the top.

CLASSIC LASAGNA

SERVES 8   641 CALS PER SERVING

Ingredients

Meat sauce

2 tbsp olive oil

2lb (1kg) ground beef

⅓ cup all-purpose flour

1¼ cups beef stock

1 x 14oz (400g) can
  chopped tomatoes

6 celery stalks, sliced

2 onions, chopped

2 large garlic cloves, crushed

¼ cup tomato paste

1 tsp sugar

salt and black pepper

For the white sauce

4 tbsp butter

⅓ cup all-purpose flour

2½ cups milk

1 tsp Dijon mustard

¼ tsp grated nutmeg

For the lasagna

4oz (125g) aged Cheddar
  cheese, grated

1oz (30g) Parmesan
  cheese, grated

6oz (175g) no-boil lasagna

chopped parsley to garnish

1 Preheat the oven to 375°F (190°C). Make the meat sauce: heat the oil in a saucepan, add the beef, and cook, stirring, until browned.

2 Sprinkle in the flour and stir for 1 minute, then add the stock, tomatoes, celery, onions, garlic, tomato paste, and sugar. Season with salt and pepper and bring to a boil. Cover and simmer for 1 hour.

3 Meanwhile, make the white sauce: melt the butter in a saucepan, sprinkle in the flour, and cook, stirring, for 1 minute. Remove from the heat and gradually blend in the milk. Bring to a boil, stirring until the mixture thickens. Simmer for 2–3 minutes. Stir in the mustard and nutmeg, and season with salt and pepper.

4 Spoon one-third of the meat sauce into a large shallow ovenproof dish, and cover with one-third of the white sauce and one-third of the Cheddar and Parmesan cheeses. Arrange half of the lasagna in a single layer. Repeat the layers, finishing with the Cheddar and Parmesan cheeses.

5 Bake in the oven for 45–60 minutes until the pasta is tender and the topping is a golden brown color. Serve at once, sprinkled with parsley.

JALAPEÑO DEEP-DISH
pizza

SERVES 8   450 CALS PER SLICE

Ingredients

Dough

3½ cups bread flour

1 x ¼oz (7g) package fast-acting dried yeast

½ tsp salt

2 tbsp olive oil, plus extra for greasing

For the pizza

½ cup tomato sauce

1 x 14oz (400g) can chopped tomatoes, drained

2oz (60g) pepperoni, sliced

10oz (300g) mozzarella cheese, grated

2oz (60g) Parmesan cheese, grated

2 tbsp sliced pickled jalapeños (from a can or jar)

Special equipment

deep-dish 14in (35cm) round pizza pan

1 Make the dough: mix the flour, yeast, salt, and 2 tablespoons oil in a large bowl. Add enough lukewarm water (about 1¼ cups) to make a soft, sticky dough. Knead on a lightly floured surface for 5–10 minutes until smooth and elastic.

2 Put into a large oiled bowl, turn to coat with the oil, cover with oiled plastic wrap, and let rise in a warm place for 1 hour or until doubled in size. Preheat the oven to 475°F (240°C).

3 Lightly oil the pizza pan. Knock back the dough on a floured surface, roll out, and shape into a 14in (35cm) round. Put into the pan and shape the edges to form a rim.

4 Spread the tomato sauce over the base. Top with the tomatoes and pepperoni. Sprinkle with the mozzarella, Parmesan, and jalapeños.

5 Bake for 10–15 minutes until the crust is golden and the cheese topping melted. Serve hot.

CALZONE

SERVES 4   899 CALS PER SERVING

Ingredients

Dough

3½ cups bread flour

1 x ¼oz (7g) package
  fast-acting dried yeast

3 tbsp olive oil, plus extra
  for greasing

beaten egg to seal and glaze

Filling

3 tbsp olive oil

2 large onions, sliced

1 tsp balsamic vinegar

3 Romano or red bell
  peppers, halved, seeded,
  and chopped

8oz (250g) cremini
  mushrooms, thickly sliced

salt and black pepper

1 x 14oz (400g) can
  chopped tomatoes,
  drained

¼ cup tomato paste

1oz (30g) pitted black
  olives, halved

6oz (175g) aged Cheddar
  cheese, grated

1 Make the dough: put the flour, yeast, olive oil, and 1¼ cup lukewarm water into an electric mixer and mix with the dough hook for about 5 minutes until a dough forms. If making the dough by hand, put the dry ingredients into a large bowl, add the oil and water, and mix with your hands.

2 Knead the dough on a lightly floured surface for 5–10 minutes until smooth, shape into a ball, and place in a lightly oiled large bowl. Cover with oiled plastic wrap and let rise in a warm place for 1–1½ hours or until doubled in size. Knock back the dough on a lightly floured surface and knead until smooth. Cut into 4 equal pieces and roll out each piece to a 9in (23cm) round. Preheat the oven to 475°F (240°C).

3 Make the filling: heat 2 tablespoons of the olive oil in a frying pan, add the onions, and cook over high heat for 1 minute. Turn the heat down to low, cover, and cook for 15 minutes or until the onions are soft. Remove the lid, increase the heat to high, and cook for a few minutes, stirring frequently, to evaporate any liquid. Transfer the onions to a bowl, add the vinegar, and mix. Heat the remaining olive oil in the frying pan, add the peppers, and cook for 4 minutes. Add the mushrooms and cook for 2–3 minutes until just cooked, then drain. Mix the peppers and mushrooms with the onions, season, and let cool.

4 Mix the drained tomatoes and tomato paste together in a bowl. Spread one-quarter of this mixture over one half of each piece of dough. Top with one-quarter of the vegetable mixture and one-quarter of the olives and cheese. Season well. Brush the edges of the dough with beaten egg and fold each round in half to enclose the filling. Press and crimp the edges together to seal.

5 Lay the calzone on an oiled baking sheet and brush with beaten egg. Bake for about 15 minutes until light golden brown and crisp. Serve hot or warm.

VEGETARIAN
stacked enchiladas

SERVES 6   242 CALS PER SERVING

Ingredients

Mexican tomato sauce

1 tbsp olive oil

½ small onion, finely chopped

1 jalapeño, halved, seeded, and finely chopped

1 garlic clove, crushed

1 x 14oz (400g) can chopped tomatoes

grated zest of ½ lime

2 tbsp chopped fresh cilantro

salt and black pepper

For the enchiladas

4 large flour tortillas, about 9in (23cm) in diameter

1 x 6oz (175g) can red kidney beans, drained

2oz (60g) feta cheese, grated

2oz (60g) Cheddar cheese, grated

1 tbsp olive oil

guacamole to serve

1 Make the tomato sauce: heat the oil in a pan; add the onion, jalapeño, and garlic; and cook over high heat for a few minutes. Add the tomatoes and simmer without a lid over low heat, stirring from time to time, for about 10 minutes until the mixture is fairly thick (the consistency of chutney). If it is still a little runny, reduce it by boiling over high heat, stirring continuously. Add the lime zest and cilantro, and season with salt and pepper.

2 Take 1 tortilla and spread half of the tomato sauce over it to within 1in (2.5cm) of the edge. Top with half of the red kidney beans and sprinkle with half of both the cheeses. Put another tortilla on top and press down a little with your hand so the 2 tortillas are sandwiched together. Make a separate tortilla sandwich (enchilada) with the remaining ingredients.

3 Heat the oil in a frying pan with a wide base so the tortillas can fit in flat. Cook each enchilada for 3–4 minutes on each side or until the tortillas are golden brown and crisp, the filling is hot, and the cheese is melted. Slice each enchilada into 6 wedges to serve with guacamole.

MIXED BEAN
bake

SERVES 6   376 CALS PER SERVING

Ingredients

2 tbsp olive oil

3 large leeks, trimmed and sliced

1 garlic clove, crushed

8oz (250g) mushrooms, sliced

1 x 14oz (400g) can adzuki or red kidney beans, drained and rinsed

1 x 14oz (400g) can lima beans, drained and rinsed

1 x 14oz (400g) can chopped tomatoes

3 tbsp tomato paste

4 tbsp chopped parsley

salt and black pepper

Cheese sauce

2 tbsp butter

3 tbsp all-purpose flour

1¼ cups milk

1 large egg, beaten

4oz (125g) Cheddar cheese, grated

1 Preheat the oven to 375°F (190°C). Heat the olive oil in a large saucepan. Add the leeks and cook gently, stirring, for a few minutes until softened but not colored. Lift out with a slotted spoon and set aside.

2 Add the garlic and mushrooms and cook, stirring occasionally, for about 5 minutes. Add the canned beans, tomatoes, tomato paste, and 3 tablespoons of the parsley. Season with salt and pepper. Bring to a boil, cover, and simmer very gently for about 20 minutes.

3 Meanwhile, make the cheese sauce: melt the butter in a small saucepan, add the flour, and cook, stirring, for 1 minute. Remove the pan from the heat and gradually blend in the milk. Bring to a boil, stirring constantly until the mixture thickens. Simmer for 2–3 minutes, then let cool slightly. Stir in the egg and cheese and season with salt and black pepper.

4 Transfer the bean mixture to an ovenproof dish and arrange the leeks on top. Pour the cheese sauce over the leeks and bake for 30 minutes or until the top is golden. Serve hot, sprinkled with the remaining parsley.

MUSHROOM
Stroganoff

SERVES 4   177 CALS PER SERVING

Ingredients

¾oz (20g) dried
   mushrooms (porcini)

2 tbsp olive oil

1 onion, chopped

1 garlic clove, crushed

1lb (500g) cremini
   mushrooms

2 red bell peppers, halved,
   seeded, and sliced

2 tsp paprika

salt and black pepper

3 tbsp cornstarch

1¼ cups cold
   vegetable stock

1 x 14oz (400g) can
   artichoke hearts, drained

2 tbsp dry white or red wine

1 tbsp tomato paste

low-fat crème fraîche or
   plain yogurt to serve

1 Soak the dried mushrooms in ¾ cup warm water for 20 minutes, then drain and reserve the soaking water.

2 Heat the oil in a Dutch oven, add the onion and garlic, and cook for 3–5 minutes until softened.

3 Add the mushrooms, peppers, and paprika and season with salt and pepper. Cook, stirring, for 5 minutes. Mix the cornstarch and stock; add to the pan with the artichokes, wine, mushroom water, and tomato paste; and bring to a boil. Simmer gently for 10–15 minutes. Taste for seasoning. Serve hot, with crème fraîche or yogurt.

VARIATION
MUSHROOM
vol-au-vent

When cooking the mushrooms, increase the heat to reduce and thicken the sauce. Warm through a premade large vol-au-vent shell or puff pastry and fill with the hot mushroom Stroganoff.

EGGPLANT
parmigiana

SERVES 6   516 CALS PER SERVING

Ingredients

3lb (1.5kg) eggplant

2 large eggs, lightly beaten

⅓ cup all-purpose flour

3 tbsp olive oil, or more
  if needed

2 onions, chopped

3 x 14oz (400g) cans
  chopped tomatoes,
  drained

1 x 5oz (140g) can
  tomato paste

2 garlic cloves, crushed

2 tbsp chopped fresh basil

¼ tsp granulated sugar

salt and black pepper

11oz (310g) mozzarella
  cheese, sliced

4oz (125g) Parmesan
  cheese, grated

1 Cut the eggplant into ½in (1cm) slices. Dip into the beaten eggs, then into the flour, shaking off any excess.

2 Heat 1 tablespoon olive oil in a large frying pan, add the eggplant slices in batches, and cook for 3–4 minutes on each side until golden, adding more oil between batches if necessary. Lift out with a slotted spoon and drain on paper towels. Preheat the oven to 375°F (190°C).

3 Heat another tablespoon of olive oil in a saucepan, add the onions, and cook gently until soft. Stir in the tomatoes, tomato paste, garlic, and basil. Bring to a boil, then simmer for 10–15 minutes until thickened. Add the sugar and season with salt and pepper.

4 Spoon some of the tomato mixture into a shallow ovenproof dish and cover with a layer of eggplant slices, then with a layer each of mozzarella and Parmesan. Continue layering, finishing with tomato mixture, mozzarella, and Parmesan.

5 Bake for 15–20 minutes until the cheese is lightly browned.

ITALIAN STUFFED
zucchini

SERVES 4　　　437 CALS PER SERVING

Ingredients

4 large zucchini

2 tbsp butter

2 tbsp olive oil, plus
　extra for greasing

1 small onion,
　finely chopped

4 ripe tomatoes,
　finely chopped

¼ cup chopped fresh basil

salt and black pepper

2 tbsp capers, drained
　and coarsely chopped

8oz (250g) Fontina
　cheese, grated

1　Preheat the oven to 350°F (180°C). Cut the zucchini in half lengthwise. Scoop out the flesh and chop finely.

2　Melt the butter with 1 tablespoon of the olive oil in a saucepan.

3　When the butter is foaming, add the onion and cook gently, stirring occasionally, for 3–5 minutes until softened but not colored.

4　Add the zucchini flesh, tomatoes, and basil and season with salt and pepper. Cook, stirring, for 5 minutes.

5　Brush the insides of the zucchini shells with the remaining oil and arrange in a lightly oiled shallow ovenproof dish. Bake the shells for 5–10 minutes.

6　Divide half of the tomato mixture among the zucchini shells. Cover with the chopped capers and a thin layer of cheese. Spoon over the remaining tomato mixture and top with the remaining cheese. Return to the oven and bake for 10–15 minutes until the cheese topping is bubbling.

POLENTA
with grilled vegetables

SERVES 6   319 CALS PER SERVING

Ingredients

1 cup polenta

2 tbsp butter

2 zucchini, halved and thickly sliced lengthwise

2 tomatoes, cored and sliced

1 fennel bulb, trimmed and quartered lengthwise

1 red onion, thickly sliced

melted butter for brushing

Marinade

¼ cup olive oil

2 tbsp red wine vinegar

3 garlic cloves, chopped

2–3 tbsp chopped parsley

salt and black pepper

1 Put the polenta into a saucepan, cover with ¾ cup cold water, and let stand for 5 minutes.

2 Add 2½ cups boiling salted water to the pan, return to a boil, and stir for 10–15 minutes until smooth and thickened.

3 Sprinkle a baking sheet with water. Stir the butter into the polenta, then spread the mixture over the pan in a ½in (1cm) layer. Let cool.

4 Combine the marinade ingredients in a bowl. Add the zucchini, tomatoes, fennel, and onion. Cover and marinate in the refrigerator for 30 minutes.

5 Lift the vegetables out of the marinade and cook over a hot grill for 2–3 minutes on each side. Cut the polenta into strips and cook over the grill, brushing with melted butter, for 1–2 minutes on each side until golden. Serve hot.

SPINACH GNOCCHI
with tomato sauce

SERVES 4   738 CALS PER SERVING

Ingredients

2lb (1kg) spinach leaves

12oz (350g) ricotta cheese

3 large eggs

¼ cup grated
    Parmesan cheese

pinch of grated nutmeg

salt and black pepper

⅓–½ cup all-purpose flour

Tomato sauce

2 tbsp butter

1 small onion, chopped

1 small carrot, chopped

⅓ cup all-purpose flour

1 x 14oz (400g) can
    chopped tomatoes

1¼ cups vegetable stock

1 bay leaf

1 tsp granulated sugar

To serve

9 tbsp butter

grated Parmesan cheese
    and Parmesan shavings

1 Wash the spinach and put into a saucepan with only the water remaining on the leaves. Cook over low heat until just wilted. Drain the spinach throughly, squeezing to remove any excess water.

2 Put the spinach, ricotta, eggs, Parmesan, and nutmeg into a food processor; season with salt and pepper; and purée until smooth. Turn into a bowl and gradually add flour until the mixture just holds its shape.

3 Using 2 teaspoons, form the mixture into 20 oval shapes. Cover and chill in the refrigerator for 1 hour.

4 Make the tomato sauce: melt the butter in a pan, add the onion and carrot, and cook for 10 minutes or until softened. Sprinkle in the flour and cook, stirring, for 1 minute. Add the tomatoes, stock, bay leaf, and sugar; season with salt and pepper; and bring to a boil. Cover and simmer for 30 minutes. Purée in a food processor until smooth. Keep hot.

5 Cook the gnocchi in batches in boiling salted water for about 5 minutes or until they float to the surface. Lift out and keep hot. Melt the butter and pour over the gnocchi. Serve the gnocchi hot, with the tomato sauce, grated Parmesan, and Parmesan shavings.

COUSCOUS
with roasted bell peppers

SERVES 4–6   279–418 CALS PER SERVING

Ingredients

1 large red bell pepper

1 large yellow bell pepper

2 cups couscous

2½ cups hot vegetable stock

2 tbsp olive oil

½ cup blanched almonds

2 zucchini, sliced

1 large red onion, chopped

1 large carrot, thinly sliced

1–2 garlic cloves, crushed

1 x 14oz (400g) can
  chickpeas, drained
  and rinsed

1 tsp ground cumin

½ tsp curry powder

¼–½ tsp crushed dried
  red chiles

salt and black pepper

chopped cilantro
  to garnish

1 Cook the peppers under a hot broiler, 4in (10cm) from the heat, for 10 minutes or until charred. Seal in a plastic bag and let cool.

2 Put the couscous into a bowl and stir in the hot stock. Cover and let stand for 10 minutes.

3 Meanwhile, heat the oil in a large frying pan, add the almonds, and cook gently, stirring, for 3 minutes or until lightly browned. Lift out with a slotted spoon and drain on paper towels.

4 Add the zucchini, onion, carrot, and garlic to the pan and cook, stirring, for about 5 minutes.

5 Stir in the chickpeas, cumin, curry powder, and crushed chiles and cook, stirring occasionally, for another 5 minutes. Stir in the couscous and cook for 3–4 minutes until heated through. Season to taste.

6 Remove the skins, cores, and seeds from the charred peppers and cut the flesh into thin strips.

7 Divide the couscous among warmed serving plates and arrange the pepper strips on top. Serve at once, sprinkled with the almonds and chopped cilantro.

SPICED EGGPLANT
with filo crust

SERVES 6   569 CALS PER SERVING

Ingredients

2 tbsp olive oil

2 large onions, chopped

2 tbsp mild curry paste

2 eggplant, cut into ½in (1cm) cubes

2 red bell peppers, halved, seeded, and diced

salt and black pepper

1 cup dried red lentils

8oz (250g) Emmentaler (or Swiss) cheese, cubed

10oz (300g) filo pastry

4 tbsp melted butter

mixed-greens salad to serve

Special equipment

10½in (26cm) springform cake pan

1 Preheat the oven to 375°F (190°C). Heat the oil in a large saucepan or deep frying pan. Cook the onions over low heat, stirring occasionally, for 3–5 minutes until softened. Stir in the curry paste and cook for 2 minutes.

2 Add the eggplant and the red bell peppers and cook for 10–15 minutes until soft. Season with salt and pepper and let cool.

3 Meanwhile, put the lentils into a pan, cover with water, and bring to a boil. Simmer for 15 minutes or until just soft. Drain and cool.

4 Stir the lentils and cubed cheese into the eggplant mixture. Taste for seasoning.

5 Using two-thirds of the filo, line the bottom and sides of the cake pan, brushing each sheet with melted butter, and letting them overhang the rim of the pan. Spoon in the eggplant mixture and fold the filo over the top. Brush the remaining filo with butter, crumple, and arrange on top.

6 Bake for 40 minutes or until the pastry is golden. Serve hot accompanied by a mixed-greens salad.

Cook's know-how

If you are short on time, omit the filo. Spread the eggplant, pepper, and lentil mixture in a baking dish and grate the cheese over the top.

VEGGIE BURGERS

SERVES 6   134 CALS PER SERVING

Ingredients

3 tsp butter

4oz (125g) cremini mushrooms, finely chopped

1 small leek, finely chopped

1 small jalapeño, halved, seeded, and finely chopped

1 tsp sugar

1 garlic clove, crushed

2 x 14oz (400g) cans lima beans or cannellini beans (or use one of each), drained and rinsed

all-purpose flour for coating

salt and black pepper

¼ cup olive or sunflower oil

Dressed lettuce

¼ cup reduced-calorie mayonnaise

2 tbsp Dijon mustard

dash of lemon juice

½ small head iceberg lettuce, finely shredded

1 small onion, thinly sliced

1 Melt the butter in a frying pan, add the mushrooms and leek, and cook over high heat for 2–3 minutes until fairly soft. Add the jalapeño, sugar, and garlic and stir-fry for 2–3 minutes. Add the beans and cook, stirring, for 1 minute.

2 Remove from the heat, season well, and mash with a potato masher until the beans are broken into a rough mixture with no large lumps. Shape into 6 burgers.

3 Spinkle some flour onto a plate and season with salt and pepper. Coat both sides of each burger in flour.

4 Heat the oil in a frying pan, add the burgers, and cook for about 3–4 minutes on each side until golden brown and heated through.

5 Make the dressed lettuce: combine the mayonnaise, mustard, and lemon juice. Stir in the lettuce and onion. Serve the burgers in buns with the dressed lettuce and some red onion slices.

FALAFEL
with sesame yogurt sauce

SERVES 6   326 CALS PER SERVING

Ingredients

1 x 14oz (400g) can chickpeas, drained and rinsed

6 scallions, chopped

¾ cup fresh bread crumbs

1 large egg

grated zest and juice of ½ lemon

1 garlic clove, coarsely chopped

2 tbsp coarsely chopped fresh cilantro

2 tbsp coarsely chopped parsley

1 tbsp tahini paste

1 tsp ground coriander

1 tsp ground cumin

½ tsp ground cinnamon

pinch of cayenne pepper

salt and black pepper

sunflower oil for frying

chopped fresh cilantro to garnish

warmed mini pita breads to serve

Sesame yogurt sauce

¼ cup plain yogurt

2 tbsp olive oil

1 tbsp lemon juice

1 tbsp tahini paste

_1_ Put the chickpeas into a food processor; add the scallions, bread crumbs, egg, lemon zest and juice, garlic, cilantro, parsley, tahini, ground coriander, cumin, cinnamon, and cayenne pepper; and season with salt and pepper. Purée until smooth.

_2_ Transfer to a bowl, cover, and let stand for at least 30 minutes.

_3_ Meanwhile, make the sesame yogurt sauce: in a bowl, combine the yogurt, oil, lemon juice, tahini, and salt and pepper to taste.

_4_ With dampened hands, shape the falafel mixture into balls about the size of a walnut, then flatten them into patties.

_5_ Pour enough oil into a nonstick frying pan to just cover the base and heat until hot. Shallow-fry the falafel in batches for 2–3 minutes on each side until golden. Lift out and drain on paper towels. Garnish with cilantro and serve warm with mini pita breads and sesame yogurt sauce.

PEKING TOFU
with plum sauce

SERVES 6   269 CALS PER SERVING

Ingredients

1 store-bought package moo shu pancakes (wrappers)

sunflower oil, for frying

8oz (250g) firm tofu, cut into ½in (1.5cm) cubes

6 scallions, trimmed and cut into matchsticks

¼ cucumber, peeled, seeded, and cut into matchsticks

Plum sauce

8oz (250g) dark red plums, halved and pitted

1 small apple, peeled, cored, and sliced

1 fresh red chile, halved, seeded, and finely chopped

½ cup granulated sugar

¼ cup white wine vinegar

1 Make the plum sauce: put the plums, apple, chile, sugar, vinegar, and 2 tablespoons water into a pan. Heat gently to dissolve the sugar, then bring to a boil. Partially cover and simmer gently for about 30–40 minutes until the fruits have cooked down and only a little liquid remains. Remove from the heat and let cool.

2 Pour enough oil into a nonstick frying pan to cover the base. Heat until hot, then fry the tofu for 3–4 minutes until golden brown all over, turning carefully. Remove and drain on paper towels.

3 To serve, spread a pancake with a little plum sauce; top with a little crispy fried tofu, scallions, and cucumber; and roll up to eat.

RED LENTIL
and coconut curry

SERVES 6   481 CALS PER SERVING

Ingredients

1½ cups red lentils

1in (2.5cm) piece of fresh
    ginger, peeled and grated

1½ fresh jalapeños, halved,
    seeded, and finely
    chopped

4 garlic cloves

½ cup coconut milk

½ tsp turmeric

1 tbsp lemon juice

salt

2 tbsp butter

4 tsp black mustard seeds

1 Put the lentils into a pan and add 3¾ cups water. Bring to a boil and simmer for about 20 minutes or until tender.

2 Using a mortar and pestle, crush the ginger, two-thirds of the jalapeños, and 2 garlic cloves until smooth. Add to the lentils.

3 Add the coconut milk, turmeric, lemon juice, and a pinch of salt. Cook gently, stirring, until the coconut dissolves, then increase the heat and cook for 5 minutes or until any excess liquid has evaporated. Taste for seasoning.

4 Crush the remaining garlic and set aside. Melt the butter in a frying pan and add the mustard seeds. As soon as they begin to pop, remove the frying pan from the heat and stir in the crushed garlic and the chopped chile. Serve the lentils with the mustard seeds, grated coconut, and chopped jalapeños on top.

SIDES

BOSTON
baked beans

SERVES 6–8   325–433 CALS PER SERVING

Ingredients

12oz (350g) dried
   navy beans

¼ cup dark brown sugar

2 tbsp tomato paste

2 tsp blackstrap molasses

2 tsp corn syrup

2 tsp mustard powder

2 tsp salt

black pepper

8oz (250g) thick-cut bacon,
   cut into 1in (2.5cm) cubes

3 onions, quartered

1 Put the navy beans into a large bowl, cover with plenty of cold water, and soak overnight.

2 Preheat the oven to 275°F (140°C). Drain the beans and rinse under cold running water. Put the beans into a saucepan, cover with cold water, and bring to a boil. Boil rapidly for 10 minutes, then partially cover the pan and simmer for 30 minutes. Drain and set aside.

3 Put the sugar, tomato paste, blackstrap molasses, corn syrup, and mustard powder into a large Dutch oven. Season with salt and pepper and heat gently, stirring constantly.

4 Add the bacon and onions to the pot with the drained beans and 2½ cups water. Bring to a boil, cover tightly, and cook in the oven, stirring occasionally, for 4½–5 hours. Taste for seasoning before serving.

SPICED YAMS

SERVES 4   381 CALS PER SERVING

Ingredients

3 tbsp butter

2 garlic cloves, crushed

2 yams, total weight 2lb (1kg), trimmed but unpeeled, cubed

1 tsp mild chili powder

¼ tsp paprika

¼ tsp ground cinnamon

1 x 7oz (200g) can chopped tomatoes

salt

plain yogurt and chopped parsley to serve

1 Melt the butter in a large pan. When it is foaming, add the garlic and cook gently, stirring occasionally, for 1–2 minutes until soft but not colored.

2 Add the yams to the pan and toss over medium to high heat for 1–2 minutes.

3 Stir in the chili powder, paprika, and cinnamon, then add the tomatoes and cook the mixture over medium heat for 1–2 minutes.

4 Season with salt, cover, and simmer for 15–20 minutes until the yams are tender. Turn the yams occasionally with an offset spatula, but do not stir or they will break up. Serve hot, topped with yogurt and parsley.

CAULIFLOWER
and broccoli with cheese

SERVES 4   513 CALS PER SERVING

Ingredients

1 head of cauliflower, weighing about 1lb (500g)

1 head of broccoli, weighing about 1lb (500g)

salt and black pepper

butter for greasing

2oz (60g) aged Cheddar cheese, grated, to serve

Cheese sauce

4 tbsp butter

½ cup all-purpose flour

2½ cups milk

2oz (60g) Parmesan cheese, grated

2oz (60g) aged Cheddar cheese, grated

2 tsp Dijon mustard

1   Preheat the oven to 400°F (200°C). Trim off and discard any thick, woody cauliflower and broccoli stalks. Break the heads into large florets, then cut off the thin, tender stalks and reserve.

2   Bring a saucepan of salted water to a boil. Add the cauliflower florets with all of the reserved stalks and bring back to a boil. Boil for 2 minutes, then add the broccoli florets and boil for another 2 minutes, or until the vegetables are just cooked but still firm to the bite (they should not be soft). Drain and rinse under cold running water. Drain again, then spread out in a buttered, shallow ovenproof dish with the florets facing upward.

3   Make the cheese sauce: melt the butter in a saucepan, sprinkle in the flour, and cook, stirring, for 1 minute. Remove from the heat and gradually blend in the milk. Bring to a boil, stirring constantly until thickened. Simmer for 2–3 minutes, remove from the heat, and stir in the Parmesan and Cheddar cheeses. Add the mustard, season with salt and pepper, and stir until combined.

4   Pour the sauce over the vegetables and sprinkle with the Cheddar cheese. Bake for 20 minutes or until golden and bubbling. Serve hot.

CREAMED
spinach

SERVES 4   250 CALS PER SERVING

Ingredients

1½lb (750g) fresh
  spinach leaves

3 tbsp butter

½ cup full-fat crème fraîche

¼ tsp grated nutmeg

salt and black pepper

1–2 tbsp grated
  Parmesan cheese

1 Cut any coarse outer leaves and stalks off the spinach and discard, then wash the spinach thoroughly in plenty of cold water.

2 Melt the butter in a saucepan, add the spinach, and stir until it has absorbed the butter.

3 Add half of the crème fraîche, season with the nutmeg and salt and pepper, and heat through.

4 Transfer to a shallow ovenproof dish, pour the remaining crème fraîche on top, and sprinkle with grated Parmesan. Put under a hot broiler for a few minutes until lightly browned. Serve hot.

AROMATIC
Brussels sprouts

SERVES 6–8   94–125 CALS PER SERVING

Ingredients

2lb (1kg) Brussels sprouts

salt and black pepper

3 tbsp butter

2 tsp mustard seeds

1 tbsp lemon juice

1 Cut a cross in the base of each sprout and simmer the sprouts in boiling salted water for 5–10 minutes until just tender. Drain.

2 Melt the butter in a large saucepan, add the mustard seeds, cover, and cook over low heat for 1–2 minutes until the mustard seeds have stopped popping and the butter is lightly browned. Do not let the butter burn.

3 Add the sprouts to the pan, tossing to heat them through and coat in the mustard-seed butter. Add the lemon juice, season with salt and pepper, and serve at once.

GLAZED CARROTS
and turnips

SERVES 4   115 CALS PER SERVING

Ingredients

12oz (350g) carrots, cut into 2in (5cm) strips

12oz (350g) baby turnips

1¼ cups chicken stock

2 tbsp butter

1 tsp granulated sugar

salt and black pepper

1 tbsp mixed chopped fresh mint and parsley

1 Put the vegetables into a pan with the stock, butter, and sugar. Season with salt and pepper and bring to a boil. Cover and cook for about 10 minutes until the vegetables are almost tender.

2 Remove the lid and boil rapidly until the liquid in the pan has evaporated and formed a glaze on the vegetables. Stir in the herbs and serve hot.

**Summer peas
and beans**

Such a summer treat,
homegrown beans and
peas are hugely popular
and make a great
combination.

SUMMER PEAS
and beans

SERVES 6–8   80–107 CALS PER SERVING

Ingredients

8oz (250g) shelled fresh
  fava beans (they must
  be young)

salt and black pepper

8oz (250g) shelled peas
  (they must be young)

8oz (250g) green
  beans, halved

2 tbsp butter

2 tbsp chopped fresh mint,
  plus extra to garnish

1 Cook the fava beans in a saucepan of boiling salted water for a
few minutes until just tender. Add the peas and green beans and
cook for another 5–10 minutes or until tender (the timing depends
on their freshness).

2 Drain all the vegetables and return to the pan. Add the butter
and mint and stir until the butter melts. Taste for seasoning
and serve hot, garnished with fresh mint.

ROASTED FENNEL
and sweet potato gratin

SERVES 4–6   208–312 CALS PER SERVING

Ingredients

2 large fennel bulbs

1lb (500g) sweet potatoes

salt and black pepper

4 tbsp butter

3oz (90g) Parmesan
   cheese, grated

1   Preheat the oven to 425°F (220°C). Cut each fennel bulb lengthwise in half, then cut each half lengthwise into 3 pieces, keeping the root ends intact. Peel the sweet potatoes and cut the flesh into 1½in (3.5cm) cubes.

2   Bring a saucepan of salted water to a boil. Add the fennel, bring back to a boil, and boil for 7 minutes. Add the sweet potatoes and boil for another 3 minutes. Drain the vegetables, rinse under cold running water, and dry well.

3   Melt the butter in the saucepan and return the vegetables to the pan. Toss to coat in the butter and season with salt and pepper.

4   Transfer the mixture into a shallow ovenproof dish, level the surface, and sprinkle with the cheese. Roast for 20–25 minutes until golden brown. Serve hot.

ASPARAGUS
with Parmesan

SERVES 4   215 CALS PER SERVING

Ingredients

1¼lb (625g) asparagus

3oz (90g) Parmesan
   cheese, grated

lemon wedges and flat-leaf
   parsley sprigs to garnish

Marinade

2 tbsp olive oil

2 tsp white wine vinegar

3 garlic cloves, crushed

salt and black pepper

1 Preheat the oven to 400°F (200°C). Trim the woody ends from the asparagus. Make the marinade: in a shallow dish, combine the oil, vinegar, garlic, a pinch of salt, and plenty of pepper.

2 Roll the asparagus in the marinade, cover, and marinate for 15 minutes.

3 Sprinkle the Parmesan onto a plate. Roll the asparagus in the Parmesan, then arrange in a single layer in a large ovenproof dish.

4 Pour any remaining marinade over the asparagus and roast in the oven for 10–15 minutes until lightly browned and sizzling hot. Garnish with the lemon wedges and parsley sprigs and serve hot.

Cook's know-how

To save time, you can omit the marinating and cook the asparagus on a ridged cast-iron grill pan. The charred stripes from the pan will boost the flavor of the asparagus and make it look attractive, too.

HERBED
roasted tomatoes

SERVES 4   106 CALS PER SERVING

Ingredients

1lb (500g) cherry tomatoes

fresh herb sprig to garnish

Herb butter

3 tbsp butter, softened

2 tbsp chopped fresh herbs (e.g., cilantro, basil, flat-leaf parsley)

1 garlic clove, crushed

½ tsp lemon juice

salt and black pepper

1 Preheat the oven to 450°F (230°C). Arrange the tomatoes in a single layer in an ovenproof dish. Roast for 15–20 minutes until the tomatoes are tender but still retain their shape.

2 Meanwhile, make the herb butter: put the butter into a small bowl and beat in the herbs, garlic, and lemon juice. Season with salt and pepper. Garnish with the herb sprig and serve hot, dotted with the herb butter.

RATATOUILLE

SERVES 4–6   157–236 CALS PER SERVING

Ingredients

¼ cup olive oil

1 large onion, sliced

1 large garlic clove, crushed

1 large eggplant, cut into
  ½in (1cm) slices

4 zucchini, sliced

6 juicy ripe tomatoes, sliced

1 large red bell pepper,
  halved, seeded, and sliced

1 tsp granulated sugar

salt and black pepper

1 tbsp chopped fresh
  basil to garnish

1 Heat the olive oil in a large frying pan, add the onion and garlic,
and cook gently, stirring occasionally, for 3–5 minutes until softened.

2 Add the eggplant slices, cover, and simmer gently for 20 minutes.

3 Add the zucchini, tomatoes, red bell pepper, and sugar. Season
with salt and pepper. Cover and cook gently, stirring occasionally,
for 30 minutes or until the vegetables are soft.

4 Taste for seasoning and serve hot or cold, sprinkled with
the chopped fresh basil.

THREE-CHEESE
macaroni

SERVES 8   436 CALS PER SERVING

Ingredients

12oz (350g) elbow macaroni

salt and black pepper

3 tbsp butter, plus extra
   for greasing

⅓ cup all-purpose flour

3¾ cups milk

2 tsp Dijon mustard

6oz (175g) smoked Cheddar
   cheese, grated

2oz (60g) light mozzarella
   cheese, grated

3oz (90g) aged Cheddar
   cheese, grated

½ cup fresh white
   bread crumbs

1 Preheat the oven to 400°F (200°C). Cook the macaroni in boiling
salted water for 8–10 minutes until just tender. Drain and set aside.

2 Melt the butter in a large saucepan. Add the flour and cook, stirring,
for 1 minute. Remove the pan from the heat and gradually blend in
the milk. Bring to a boil, stirring constantly until the mixture thickens.
Simmer for about 5 minutes, stirring.

3 Stir in the mustard, smoked Cheddar and mozzarella cheeses,
2oz (60g) of the aged Cheddar cheese, and the cooked macaroni.
Season with salt and pepper.

4 Lightly butter a large shallow ovenproof dish and spoon in the macaroni
mixture. Sprinkle with the bread crumbs and the remaining Cheddar
cheese and bake for about 15–20 minutes until golden and bubbling.

VARIATION

CHEESE and
leek macaroni

Omit the mozzarella.
Melt 2 tbsp butter in
a saucepan, add 2–3
trimmed and sliced leeks,
and cook gently for 3–5
minutes until softened.
Add the leeks to the sauce
with the 2 Cheddar
cheeses and the cooked
and drained macaroni.

PERSIAN PILAF

SERVES 4   426 CALS PER SERVING

Ingredients

1 small cinnamon stick

2 tsp cumin seeds

6 black peppercorns

seeds of 4 cardamom
  pods, crushed

3 cloves

2 tbsp sunflower oil

1 small onion, chopped

1 tsp turmeric

1½ cups long-grain rice

5¼ cups hot vegetable or
  chicken stock

2 bay leaves, torn
  into pieces

salt and black pepper

2oz (60g) shelled pistachios,
  coarsely chopped

1oz (30g) raisins

fresh cilantro to garnish

1 Heat a heavy pan and add the cinnamon stick, cumin seeds, peppercorns, cardamom seeds, and cloves.

2 Dry-fry the spices over medium heat for 2–3 minutes until they begin to release their aromas.

3 Add the oil to the pan and, when it is hot, add the onion and turmeric. Cook gently, stirring occasionally, for about 10 minutes until the onion is softened.

4 Add the rice and stir to coat the grains in the oil. Slowly pour in the hot stock, add the bay leaves, season with salt and pepper, and bring to a boil. Lower the heat, cover, and cook very gently for about 10 minutes without lifting the lid.

5 Remove the saucepan from the heat and let stand, still covered, for about 5 minutes.

6 Add the pistachios and raisins to the pilaf and fork them in gently to fluff up the rice. Garnish with fresh cilantro, and serve immediately.

Risi e bisi

Literally translated as rice and peas, this classic Venetian dish is traditionally served with more liquid than a risotto.

RISI E BISI

SERVES 6   390 CALS PER SERVING

Ingredients

4 tbsp butter

1 onion, finely chopped

2oz (60g) prosciutto, diced, or 3oz (90g) unsmoked bacon strips, diced

2 garlic cloves, crushed

1½ cups risotto rice

10oz (300g) frozen peas

salt and black pepper

4 cups hot chicken or vegetable stock

2oz (60g) Parmesan cheese, grated, and 2 tbsp chopped parsley to garnish

1 Melt the butter in a large pan. When it is foaming, add the onion, prosciutto, and garlic and cook gently, stirring occasionally, for 3–5 minutes until the onion is soft but not colored.

2 Add the rice and stir to coat in the butter. Add the frozen peas and seasoning.

3 Pour in half of the stock and cook, stirring constantly, over low heat until it is absorbed. Add a little more stock and cook, stirring, until it has been absorbed.

4 Continue adding the stock in this way until the rice is just tender and the mixture is thick and creamy. It should take about 25 minutes.

5 Serve hot, sprinkled with the grated Parmesan cheese and chopped parsley.

POTATOES LYONNAISE

SERVES 6   246 CALS PER SERVING

Ingredients

6 tbsp butter, plus
  extra for greasing

1 large onion, sliced

2lb (1kg) Russet potatoes,
  thickly sliced

salt and black pepper

chopped parsley to garnish

1 Preheat the oven to 375°F (190°C). Lightly butter a gratin dish. Melt
  the butter in a frying pan, add the onion, and cook gently, stirring
  occasionally, for 3–5 minutes until the onions are softened but not colored.

2 Layer the potatoes and onion in the gratin dish, seasoning each layer
  with salt and pepper, and finishing with a neat layer of potatoes.

3 Pour any butter left in the frying pan over the potatoes. Bake for 1–1½
  hours until the potatoes are tender. Garnish with parsley and serve hot.

STEAK FRIES

SERVES 6   281 CALS PER SERVING

Ingredients

1½lb (750g) Russet potatoes

sunflower oil for
  deep-frying

salt, to taste

Special equipment

deep fryer

1 Cut the potatoes into 2in x ½in (5cm x 1cm) sticks, put into a bowl
of cold water, and soak for 5–10 minutes.

2 Heat the oil in a deep fryer to 325°F (170°C). Dry the fries thoroughly,
then lower them into the deep fryer, in batches if necessary, and
deep-fry for 5–6 minutes until soft and very pale golden.

3 Lift the basket out of the fryer. Increase the temperature of the oil
to 375°F (190°C). Carefully return the basket of fries to the fryer and
deep-fry for 3–4 minutes until crisp and golden brown. Lift out the basket
and drain on paper towels. Sprinkle with salt and serve hot.

VARIATION

FRENCH fries

Cut the potatoes into
2in x ¼in (5cm x 6mm)
sticks and soak as
directed. Heat the oil
as directed and deep-fry
for 4–5 minutes. Lift out
of the fryer, increase the
heat as directed, then
return and deep-fry
for 1–2 minutes. Sprinkle
with salt and serve
at once.

Cook's know-how

Good fries should be crisp and
golden on the outside and soft
and tender in the middle. The
secret is to cook the potatoes first
in medium–hot oil until tender,
then lift them out, increase the
temperature of the oil, and cook
the fries quickly to brown and crisp
the outsides. Drain well on paper
towels before serving.

POTATOES
au gratin

SERVES 8   279 CALS PER SERVING

Ingredients

butter for greasing

⅔ cup half-and-half

⅔ cup heavy cream

1 large garlic clove, crushed

2lb (1kg) Yukon gold
   potatoes, peeled

salt and black pepper

4oz (125g) Gruyère
   cheese, grated

1   Preheat the oven to 275°F (140°C). Lightly butter a shallow gratin dish. Put the half-and-half and heavy cream into a bowl, add the garlic, and stir to mix.

2   Thinly slice the potatoes, preferably with the slicing disc of a food processor.

3   Prepare the gratin (see box, below).

4   Bake for 1½ hours or until the potatoes are tender and the topping is golden brown. Serve at once.

PREPARING THE GRATIN

Arrange a layer of potatoes, slightly overlapping, in the bottom of the gratin dish. Season with salt and pepper.

Pour a little of the cream mixture over the potatoes, then sprinkle with grated cheese. Continue layering the potatoes, cream, and cheese, and adding salt and pepper, then finish with a layer of cheese.

BREADS AND
BAKED GOODS

FARMHOUSE LOAF

MAKES 1 LARGE LOAF   2,790 CALS PER LOAF

Ingredients

5 cups bread flour, plus extra for dusting

2 tbsp butter or margarine

2 tsp salt

1 x ¼oz (7g) package fast-acting dried yeast

sunflower oil for greasing

Special equipment

9 x 5in (23 x 13cm) loaf pan

1 Preheat the oven to 450°F (230°C). Put the flour into a bowl, rub in the butter with your fingertips until the mixture resembles bread crumbs, then stir in the salt and yeast. Make a well in the middle. Add enough lukewarm water (about 2 cups) to make a soft dough that is quite sticky.

2 Knead the dough on a lightly floured surface until smooth and elastic. Shape into a round and place in a lightly oiled large bowl.

3 Cover the bowl with oiled plastic wrap and let rise in a warm place for 1–1½ hours or until the dough has doubled in size.

4 Turn the dough onto a lightly floured surface and knock back with your fists. Knead vigorously for 2–3 minutes until the dough is smooth and elastic.

5 Lightly oil the loaf pan. Shape the dough to fit the pan, tucking the ends under to give a smooth top, and place in the pan. Cover loosely with oiled plastic wrap and let rise in a warm place for 30 minutes or until the dough reaches the top of the pan.

6 Lightly dust the top of the loaf with flour and bake for 30–35 minutes until golden. Turn the loaf out and tap the base: it should sound hollow if it is cooked. Let the loaf cool on a wire rack.

DINNER ROLLS

MAKES 18   95 CALS EACH

Ingredients

3⅓ cups bread flour

1 tsp salt

1 x ¼oz (7g) package
    fast-acting dried yeast

sunflower oil for greasing

1 Preheat the oven to 375°F (190°C). Put the flour into a large bowl, then stir in the salt and yeast. Make a well in the middle and pour in enough lukewarm water (about 1½ cups) to make a soft, sticky dough.

2 Knead the dough on a lightly floured surface until smooth and elastic. Shape into a round and place in a large lightly oiled bowl. Cover with oiled plastic wrap and let rise in a warm place for 1–1½ hours or until doubled in size.

3 Lightly oil 2 or 3 baking sheets. Divide the dough into 18 pieces. Shape into balls, folding the sides to the middles to form round balls. Arrange on the pans, leaving room for expansion. Cover loosely with oiled plastic wrap and let rise in a warm place for 20 minutes or until doubled in size.

4 Bake for 20 minutes or until golden. Let cool on a wire rack.

CHEESE AND HERB
bread

MAKES 1 MEDIUM LOAF

2,707 CALS PER LOAF

Ingredients

3⅓ cups bread flour, plus extra for dusting

3oz (90g) aged Cheddar cheese, grated

1oz (30g) Parmesan cheese, grated

2 tsp ground mustard

2 tbsp chopped parsley

1½ tsp salt

1 x ¼oz (7g) package fast-acting dried yeast

about 1½ cups lukewarm milk

sunflower oil for greasing

beaten egg for glazing

2 tbsp grated Cheddar cheese for sprinkling

1 Preheat the oven to 450°F (230°C). Put the flour into a large bowl and stir in the cheeses, ground mustard, parsley, salt, and yeast, mixing thoroughly. Make a well in the middle and add enough milk to make a soft, sticky dough.

2 Knead the dough on a lightly floured surface until smooth and elastic.

3 Shape the dough into a round and place in a lightly oiled bowl. Cover with oiled plastic wrap and let rise in a warm place for 1–1½ hours or until doubled in size.

4 Turn the dough onto a floured surface and knock back. Knead for 2–3 minutes until smooth and elastic.

5 Lightly flour a baking sheet. Shape the dough into a 6in (15cm) round and place on the baking sheet. Cover loosely with oiled plastic wrap and let rise in a warm place for 20–30 minutes.

6 Brush with the egg to glaze, cut a shallow cross in the top, and sprinkle with the grated Cheddar cheese. Bake for 10 minutes; reduce the oven temperature to 400°F (200°C) and bake for 20 minutes, covering the loaf loosely with foil halfway through baking if it is browning too much. Let cool on a wire rack.

POTATO BREAD

MAKES 2 SMALL LOAVES   1,002 CALS PER LOAF

Ingredients

3⅓ cups bread flour, plus extra for dusting

1 tsp salt

3 tsp butter

1 x ¼oz (7g) package fast-acting dried yeast

1 cup cold mashed potato

sunflower oil for greasing

Special equipment

2 x 8½ x 4½in (22 x 11cm) loaf pans

1 Preheat the oven to 450°F (230°C). Put the flour and salt into a large bowl, rub in the butter, then stir in the yeast. Add the potato, rubbing it loosely into the flour. Make a well in the middle of the ingredients and add enough lukewarm water (about 1 cup) to make a soft, sticky dough.

2 Knead the dough on a floured surface until smooth and elastic, then shape into a round. Place in a lightly oiled large bowl, cover with oiled plastic wrap, and let rise in a warm place for 1 hour or until doubled in size.

3 Turn the dough onto a lightly floured surface and knock back with your fists. Knead until smooth and elastic.

4 Lightly oil the loaf pans. Divide the dough in half and shape to fit the pans, tucking the ends underneath. Place in the pans. Cover loosely with oiled plastic wrap and leave in a warm place to rise for 30 minutes or until the dough reaches the tops of the pans.

5 Bake for 10 minutes; reduce the oven temperature to 400°F (200°C) and bake for 20–25 minutes until golden. Tap the bases of the loaves to see if they are cooked: they should sound hollow. Serve warm or cold.

Cook's know-how

Always add the measured liquid gradually when making dough. Recipes cannot specify exact amounts because flours vary in how much liquid they will absorb.

FOCACCIA

MAKES 1 LARGE LOAF   2,989 CALS PER LOAF

Ingredients

5 cups bread flour, plus
   extra for dusting

1 x ¼oz (7g) package
   fast-acting dried yeast

3–4 tbsp chopped
   fresh rosemary

3 tbsp olive oil, plus
   extra for greasing

2 tsp coarse sea salt

1 Preheat the oven to 375°F (190°C). Put the flour into a bowl and add the yeast and rosemary. Make a well in the middle and add the oil and enough lukewarm water (about 2 cups) to make a soft but not sticky dough. Knead the dough until smooth and elastic, then shape into a round.

2 Place the dough in a lightly oiled large bowl, cover loosely with oiled plastic wrap, and let rise in a warm place for about 1 hour or until the dough has doubled in size.

3 Turn the dough onto a lightly floured surface and knock back with your fists. Knead for 2–3 minutes until smooth. Roll out the dough to a round 2in (5cm) thick. Cover loosely with oiled plastic wrap and leave in a warm place for 1 hour or until doubled in size.

4 Brush with olive oil and sprinkle with sea salt. Bake for 20 minutes until golden. Best eaten warm.

CROISSANTS

MAKES 12   352 CALS EACH

Ingredients

3⅓ cups bread flour

½ tsp salt

21 tbsp (2 sticks + 5 tbsp) butter, at room temperature

1 x ¼oz (7g) package fast-acting dried yeast

2 tbsp granulated sugar

about ⅔ cup milk

sunflower oil for greasing

beaten egg for glazing

1 Preheat the oven to 425°F (220°C). Put the flour and salt into a large bowl, add 4 tablespoons of the butter, and rub in with your fingertips until the mixture resembles fine bread crumbs. Stir in the yeast and sugar.

2 Make a well in the middle of the dry ingredients. Mix the milk and about ⅔ cup of very hot water together, pour into the well, and mix with a wooden spoon until smooth.

3 Cover the bowl with oiled plastic wrap and chill the dough for 2 hours.

4 Meanwhile, on a sheet of parchment paper, spread out the remaining butter into a 5 x 8in (12 x 20cm) rectangle. Cover with another sheet of parchment paper and chill.

5 Roll out the dough on a floured surface into a 7 x 14in (18 x 35cm) rectangle and place the chilled butter on top so that it covers the top two-thirds of the rectangle.

6 Fold the bottom third of the dough over the middle third, and fold the top third, with the butter, over the top to form a neat parcel. Seal the edges with the edge of your hand. Wrap and chill for 30 minutes.

7 Roll out the dough parcel into a 7 x 14in (18 x 35cm) rectangle, fold into 3 as before, and seal the edges. Wrap and chill for a few hours until firm enough to roll and shape.

8 Shape the croissants (see box, opposite). Place on 2 baking sheets and leave for about 30 minutes until almost doubled in size.

9 Lightly brush the croissants with the beaten egg and bake for 12–15 minutes until crisp and golden brown. Let cool slightly before serving.

VARIATION

CHOCOLATE croissants

Make the dough. Before rolling the triangles into sausage shapes, sprinkle with 3oz (90g) semisweet chocolate chips.

SHAPING THE CROISSANT

Roll out the dough into a 14 x 21in (35 x 53cm) rectangle, and cut into 12 triangles.

Roll each triangle into a sausage shape, starting from the long side and ending with the point of the triangle.

Bend the ends of each croissant to give the traditional shape.

CINNAMON
rolls

MAKES 16   450 CALS EACH

Ingredients

6⅔ cups all-purpose flour

4 tbsp granulated sugar

1 x ¼oz (7g) package
 fast-acting dried yeast

1 tsp salt

about 1½ cups
 lukewarm milk

2 extra-large eggs,
 lightly beaten

2 tbsp butter, melted

1½ cups raisins

1 tbsp ground cinnamon

sunflower oil for greasing

milk for glazing

Glaze

2 cups confectioner's sugar

1 tsp pure vanilla extract

1 Preheat the oven to 375°F (190°C). Sift the flour and 2 tablespoons of the sugar into a bowl, then stir in the yeast and salt. Make a well in the middle; pour in the milk, eggs, and butter; and stir to make a sticky dough.

2 Knead the dough on a lightly floured surface until smooth and elastic.

3 Knead in the raisins and half of the cinnamon, then divide the dough into 16 even-sized pieces. Shape each piece into an 8–10in (20–25cm) strand, then flatten.

4 Combine the remaining sugar and cinnamon, sprinkle the mixture over the strips of dough, then roll up tightly into spirals.

5 Lightly oil 2 baking sheets. Arrange the rolls on the pans, cover loosely with oiled plastic wrap, and let rise in a warm place for about 1 hour or until doubled in size.

6 Brush the rolls with milk to glaze, then bake for 30–40 minutes until lightly browned. Transfer the rolls to a rack.

7 Meanwhile, make the glaze: in a small bowl, combine the confectioner's sugar, ¼ cup water, and vanilla extract. As soon as the cinnamon rolls come out of the oven, brush them with the glaze. Serve the rolls warm or cold with butter.

WHOLE WHEAT
drop scones

MAKES 20   55 CALS EACH

Ingredients

1 cup whole wheat flour

1 tsp baking powder

3 tbsp granulated sugar

1 large egg

¾ cup milk

sunflower oil for greasing

syrup or butter
    and jam to serve

1 Combine the flour, baking powder, and sugar in a bowl and stir to
   mix. Make a well in the middle of the dry ingredients and add the
egg and half of the milk. Beat well to make a smooth, thick batter.

2 Add enough milk to give the batter the consistency of thick cream.

3 Heat a flat grill pan or heavy frying pan and grease with oil. Drop
   spoonfuls of batter onto the hot pan, spacing them well apart.
When bubbles rise to the surface, turn scones over and cook until golden.

4 As each batch is cooked, wrap the scones in a clean kitchen towel
   to keep them soft. Serve warm, with syrup or butter and jam.

VARIATION

PLAIN
drop scones

Substitute white self-
rising flour for the whole
wheat flour, and use a
little less milk.

IRISH
soda bread

CUTS INTO 8 WEDGES   227 CALS EACH

Ingredients

3 cups all-purpose flour,
plus extra for dusting

1 tsp baking soda

1 tsp salt

1¼ cups buttermilk, or half
milk and half plain yogurt

sunflower oil for greasing

1 Preheat the oven to 400°F (200°C). Sift the flour, baking soda, and
salt into a large bowl. Pour in the buttermilk, or milk and yogurt,
and ⅓ cup water. Mix with a wooden spoon or your hands
to form a very soft dough.

2 Lightly oil a baking sheet. Turn the dough onto a lightly floured work
surface and shape into a round measuring 7in (18cm) in diameter.

3 Place the loaf on the prepared baking sheet and cut a deep
cross in the top.

4 Bake for 30 minutes. Turn the bread over and bake for another
10 minutes or until the loaf sounds hollow when tapped on
the base. Cool on a wire rack. Serve on the day of making.

CHELSEA BUNS

MAKES 12   298 CALS EACH

Ingredients

3⅓ cups bread flour

1 tsp salt

4 tbsp butter

1 x ¼oz (7g) package
   fast-acting dried yeast

2 tbsp granulated sugar

about ¾ cup lukewarm milk

1 extra-large egg, beaten

sunflower oil for greasing

¼ cup honey

Filling

4 tbsp butter

2 tbsp light brown sugar

⅓ cup golden raisins

⅓ cup currants

grated zest of 1 orange

1 tsp pumpkin pie spice

1 Preheat the oven to 425°F (220°C). Put the flour into a large bowl and stir in the salt. Rub in the butter and yeast. Stir in the sugar. Make a well in the middle, pour in the milk and egg, and mix to a soft dough.

2 Knead the dough on a lightly floured surface until smooth and elastic, then shape into a round and place in a lightly oiled large bowl. Cover with oiled plastic wrap and leave in a warm place for 1–1½ hours or until doubled in size.

3 Make the filling: cream the butter with the brown sugar. In another bowl, combine the golden raisins, currants, orange zest, and pumpkin pie spice.

4 Lightly oil a 7 x 11in (18 x 28cm) roasting pan. Turn the dough onto a lightly floured surface and knock back with your fists. Knead for 2–3 minutes until smooth.

5 Roll out into a 12in (30cm) square and dot with the butter mixture. Fold in half and roll out into a 12in (30cm) square. Sprinkle with the fruit mixture, then roll up.

6 Cut the roll into 12 pieces and arrange cut-side up in the roasting pan. Cover with oiled plastic wrap. Leave in a warm place to rise for about 30 minutes or until the pieces are touching.

7 Bake for 20–25 minutes, covering the buns loosely with foil after about 15 minutes to prevent them from browning too much. Transfer to a wire rack.

8 Warm the honey in a small pan and brush over the buns to glaze. Pull the buns apart and serve warm.

Chelsea buns

50,000 people lined up to try this new sweet, fruity dough when Chelsea buns first went on sale at the Chelsea Bun House, London, in the 18th century.

Bath buns

Dating back to the 18th century, these sweet and sticky treats were a favorite of author Jane Austen. Delicious when eaten warm.

BATH BUNS

MAKES 18   196 CALS EACH

Ingredients

3⅓ cups bread flour

¼ cup granulated sugar

1 tsp salt

1 x ¼oz (7g) package
  fast-acting dried yeast

about ⅔ cup lukewarm milk

4 tbsp butter, melted and
  cooled slightly

1 large egg and 2 large
  egg yolks, beaten

1 cup golden raisins

3oz (90g) chopped
  citrus peel

sunflower oil for greasing

Topping

1 large egg, beaten

1oz (30g) pearl sugar
  or coarsely crushed
  sugar cubes

1 Preheat the oven to 375°F (190°C). Put the flour and sugar into a large bowl and stir in the salt and yeast. Make a well in the middle and add the milk, butter, egg and egg yolks, golden raisins, and citrus peel. Mix to a soft dough.

2 Knead the dough on a lightly floured surface until smooth and elastic.

3 Shape the dough into a round and place in an oiled bowl. Cover with oiled plastic wrap and let rise in a warm place for 1–1½ hours or until the dough has doubled in size.

4 Turn the dough onto a lightly floured surface and knock back. Knead the dough for 2–3 minutes until smooth and elastic.

5 Lightly oil 2 or 3 baking sheets. Divide the dough into 18 pieces, shape into rolls, and place on the baking sheets. Cover loosely with oiled plastic wrap and let rise in a warm place for about 30 minutes or until doubled in size.

6 Brush the tops of the buns with the beaten egg and sprinkle with the sugar. Bake for 15 minutes or until golden brown.

7 Tap the bases of the buns to see if they are cooked through: they should sound hollow. Let cool on a wire rack.

DESSERTS

APPLE
Brown Betty

SERVES 6   284 CALS PER SERVING

Ingredients

2–3 tbsp butter

1½ cups stale bread crumbs

2lb (1kg) tart apples, quartered, cored, peeled, and thinly sliced

½ cup granulated sugar, plus extra for sprinkling

1 tbsp lemon juice

1–2 tsp ground cinnamon

Special equipment

deep 2-quart (2-liter) ovenproof dish

1   Preheat the oven to 400°F (200°C). Melt the butter in a frying pan. Add the bread crumbs and stir over medium heat for 5 minutes or until the crumbs are crisp and golden. Remove from the heat.

2   Toss the apples with the granulated sugar, lemon juice, and ground cinnamon.

3   Press one-quarter of the crisp bread crumbs over the bottom of the dish. Cover with half of the apple mixture and sprinkle with another one-quarter of the bread crumbs.

4   Arrange the remaining apple mixture on top of the bread crumbs, spoon over any juices, and cover with the remaining bread crumbs. Sprinkle the top of the dessert lightly with granulated sugar.

5   Cover the dish with foil. Bake for about 20 minutes.

6   Remove the foil and continue baking for another 20 minutes or until the apples are tender and the top is golden brown. Serve warm.

VARIATION

APPLE and cranberry Brown Betty

Add 6oz (175g) fresh or thawed frozen cranberries to the apple mixture. Add a little more sugar if necessary.

Cook's know-how

White or brown bread can be used for the bread crumbs. Whole wheat gives a nutty flavor, and whole grain gives an interesting texture. For best results, the bread should be about 2 days old.

CHERRIES JUBILEE

SERVES 4   162 CALS PER SERVING

Ingredients

1 x 15oz (425g) jar or can
   Morello cherries in syrup

2–3 tbsp granulated sugar

⅓ cup brandy

a few drops of
   almond extract

vanilla ice cream to serve

1 Drain the cherries, reserving ½ cup of the syrup. Put the cherries into a saucepan with the measured syrup and the sugar.

2 Heat gently, stirring, until the sugar has dissolved, then bring to a boil. Simmer for about 5 minutes until the liquid has thickened and reduced by about half.

3 Pour the brandy over the cherries and add the almond extract. Boil to evaporate the alcohol, then spoon the hot cherries and syrup over scoops of vanilla ice cream and serve at once.

VARIATION

FRESH
cherries jubilee

Replace the Morello cherries with 1lb (500g) fresh cherries. Pit the cherries and poach them in 1 cup red wine and ½ cup granulated sugar until tender. Substitute the poaching liquid for the syrup.

TIRAMISU

SERVES 8   508 CALS PER SERVING

Ingredients

1 heaping tsp instant coffee granules

3 tbsp brandy

2 large eggs

⅓ cup granulated sugar

8oz (250g) full-fat mascarpone cheese

1¼ cups heavy cream, whipped until thick

sliced poundcake

2oz (60g) dark chocolate, coarsely grated

1oz (30g) white chocolate, coarsely grated, to decorate

1 Dissolve the coffee in the ½ cup boiling water and mix with the brandy.

2 Combine the eggs and granulated sugar in a large bowl, and whisk together until thick and light and the mixture leaves a trail on the surface.

3 Put the mascarpone into a bowl and stir in a little of the egg mixture. Fold in the rest, then fold in the cream.

4 Layer the tiramisu (see box, below) with half of the poundcake slices, half the coffee and brandy mixture, half the mascarpone mixture, and half the dark chocolate.

5 Repeat the layers with the remaining ingredients, decorating the top with the grated white chocolate and the remaining grated dark chocolate. Cover and chill for at least 4 hours before serving.

LAYERING THE TIRAMISU

Line the bottom of a large glass serving bowl with half of the poundcake slices. Drizzle half of the coffee and brandy mixture over the sponges.

CHOCOLATE CHIP
cheesecake

SERVES 8   628 CALS PER SERVING

Ingredients

Crust

1½ cups muesli

6 tbsp butter, melted

3 tbsp dark brown sugar

For the cheesecake

4oz (125g) dark chocolate, broken into pieces

2 tbsp powdered gelatin

8oz (250g) full-fat cream cheese

2 large eggs, separated

¼ cup granulated sugar

⅔ cup sour cream

1oz (30g) dark chocolate chips, coarsely chopped

Decoration

1¼ cups whipping cream, whipped until stiff

chocolate curls

Special equipment

8in (20cm) loose-bottomed or springform cake pan

1   Make the crust: mix together the muesli, melted butter, and sugar and press evenly over the bottom of the pan. Chill.

2   Meanwhile, put the chocolate into a small heatproof bowl over a pan of hot water. Heat gently to melt the chocolate, stirring occasionally. Let cool.

3   Put 3 tablespoons of cold water into a heatproof bowl and sprinkle the gelatin over the top. Leave for 10 minutes until spongy. Stand the bowl in a pan of hot water and heat gently until the gelatin has dissolved.

4   Beat the cream cheese until smooth. Add the egg yolks and sugar and beat until blended. Stir in the sour cream, melted chocolate, chocolate chips, and gelatin. Mix well.

5   In a separate bowl, whisk the egg whites until stiff but not dry. Fold carefully into the chocolate mixture until evenly mixed. Pour onto the muesli base and chill until set.

6   Use a knife to loosen the side of the cheesecake from the pan, then remove the cheesecake. Slide onto a serving plate. Pipe rosettes of whipped cream (page 19) on top and decorate with chocolate curls.

Cook's know-how

Chocolate chips are convenient, but if you don't have any on hand, simply chop up a bar of dark chocolate.

CHOCOLATE
and brandy mousse

SERVES 6   585 CALS PER SERVING

Ingredients

8oz (250g) dark chocolate, broken into pieces

3 tbsp brandy

2 tbsp powdered gelatin

4 large eggs, plus 2 large egg yolks

⅓ cup granulated sugar

⅔ cup whipping cream, whipped until thick

Decoration

⅔ cup heavy or whipping cream, whipped until stiff

chocolate curls

1 Put the chocolate into a heatproof bowl with the brandy over a pan of hot water. Heat gently until melted. Let cool.

2 Put 3 tablespoons of cold water into a heatproof bowl and sprinkle the gelatin over the top. Leave for about 10 minutes until spongy. Stand the bowl in a pan of hot water and heat gently until dissolved.

3 Combine the eggs, egg yolks, and sugar in a large heatproof bowl and put over a saucepan of simmering water. Whisk with a handheld electric mixer until the egg mixture is very thick and mousselike. Whisk in the dissolved gelatin.

4 Fold the whipped cream into the cooled chocolate, then fold into the egg mixture. Carefully pour into a glass serving bowl, cover, and leave in the refrigerator until set.

5 Decorate with piped rosettes of cream and chocolate curls (page 19). Serve the mousse chilled.

Cook's know-how

Buy a good-quality dark chocolate. For the best flavor, look for a brand with at least 70% cocoa solids.

Orange panna cotta with soaked oranges

A dessert to impress. I love using oranges to add color and sweetness to this classic Italian dessert.

ORANGE PANNA COTTA
with soaked oranges

MAKES 4   782 CALS PER SERVING

Ingredients

sunflower oil for greasing

2 tsp powdered gelatin

2½ cups whipping cream

¼ cup granulated sugar

5 oranges

¼ cup orange liqueur

Special equipment

4 x 5fl oz (150ml) ramekins
or metal molds

1 Brush the molds with oil and stand them on a pan. Measure 3 tablespoons of cold water into a small bowl, sprinkle the gelatin over the top, and leave to become spongy.

2 Meanwhile, pour the cream into a saucepan and add the sugar. Finely grate the zest from the oranges and add to the pan with 2 tablespoons of the liqueur. Heat the cream until bubbles appear around the edges, stirring until the sugar has dissolved and the cream is smooth. Remove from the heat and let cool slightly.

3 Add the sponged gelatin to the warm cream and whisk until completely dissolved and smooth. Pour the cream into the prepared molds. Chill for about 6 hours, ideally overnight, until set.

4 Using a serrated knife, peel and segment the oranges, working over a bowl to catch the juice. Transfer the segments into the bowl and squeeze the thick, white membranes over the bowl to extract the remaining juice. Stir in the remaining liqueur. Chill until serving time.

5 To serve, dip each mold briefly into very hot water, then loosen the panna cotta away from the top of the mold with your fingertips and carefully turn onto a plate. Serve chilled, with a spoonful of soaked oranges alongside.

QUICK VANILLA
ice cream

SERVES 4–6   533–799 CALS PER SERVING

Ingredients

6 large eggs, separated

1 tsp pure vanilla extract

¾ cup granulated sugar

2 cups heavy cream,
  whipped until thick

1 Whisk the egg whites (at high speed if using an electric mixer) until stiff but not dry. Add the vanilla extract and the sugar, 1 teaspoon at a time, and continue whisking until the sugar has been incorporated and the egg white mixture is very stiff and glossy.

2 Put the egg yolks into a separate bowl and whisk at high speed with an electric mixer until blended thoroughly.

3 Gently fold the whipped cream and egg yolks into the egg white mixture. Turn into a large shallow freezerproof container, cover, and let the mixture freeze for 8 hours.

4 Transfer the ice cream to the refrigerator for about 10 minutes before serving so that it softens slightly. Serve with crisp wafers.

VARIATION

CAPPUCCINO
ice cream

Add 6oz (175g) fresh or thawed frozen cranberries to the apple mixture. Add a little more sugar if necessary.

VARIATION

LEMON
ice cream

Substitute granulated sugar for the vanilla sugar and add the finely grated zest and juice of 3 large lemons when folding the mixtures in step 3.

PEACH MELBA

SERVES 4   162 CALS PER SERVING

Ingredients

Melba sauce

12oz (350g) raspberries

about ¼ cup confectioner's
    sugar

For the dessert

4 ripe peaches, peeled,
    pitted, and sliced

8 scoops of vanilla
    ice cream

mint sprigs to decorate

1 Make the Melba sauce (see box, below).

2 Arrange the peach slices in 4 glass serving dishes.
Top each with 2 scoops of ice cream and some sauce.
Decorate with mint sprigs and the remaining raspberries.

MAKING MELBA SAUCE

Purée 8oz (250g) of the raspberries.
Push through a sieve to remove the seeds.
Sift the confectioner's sugar over the
purée and stir in.

CHOCOLATE CAKE

CUTS INTO 14 SLICES   391 CALS EACH

Ingredients

6 tbsp butter, melted and
  cooled slightly, plus extra
  for greasing

6 large eggs

⅔ cup granulated sugar

1 cup self-rising flour

⅓ cup cocoa powder

2 tbsp cornstarch

Filling and topping

1¼ cups heavy or whipping
  cream, whipped until thick

white chocolate curls,
  optional (page 19)

Special equipment

deep 9in (23cm) round
  cake pan

1 Preheat the oven to 350°F (180°C). Lightly butter the cake pan and
line the bottom of the pan with parchment paper.

2 Put the eggs and sugar into a large bowl and whisk together with
an electric mixer on high speed until the mixture is pale and thick
enough to leave a trail on itself when the beaters are lifted out.

3 Sift together the flour, cocoa powder, and cornstarch, and fold half
into the egg mixture. Pour half of the cooled butter around the
edge; fold in gently.

4 Repeat with the remaining flour mixture and butter, folding gently.

5 Turn the mixture into the prepared cake pan and tilt the pan to level
the surface. Bake for 35–40 minutes until the cake is well risen and
firm to the touch. Turn onto a wire rack, peel off the lining, and cool.

6 Cut the cake in half horizontally and sandwich the layers together
with half of the whipped cream. Cover the cake with a thin layer
of cream, then pipe the remainder around the top and bottom edges.

7 Press the chocolate curls over the top and side of the cake, if using.

SORBET SELECTION

Lime sorbet

SERVES 6   169 CALS PER SERVING

1 cup (250g) granulated sugar
finely grated zest and juice of 6 limes
2 egg whites
strips of lime peel to decorate

Put the sugar and 1 pint (600ml) water into a saucepan and heat gently until the sugar dissolves. Bring to a boil and boil for 2 minutes. Remove from the heat, add the lime zest, and leave to cool. Stir in the lime juice. Strain into a shallow freezerproof container and freeze for about 2 hours until just mushy. Place into a bowl and whisk gently to break down any crystals. Whisk the egg whites until stiff but not dry, then fold into the lime mixture. Freeze until firm. Transfer to the refrigerator to soften for about 30 minutes before serving, and top with strips of lime peel.

Apricot sorbet

SERVES 6   104 CALS PER SERVING

⅓ cup (90g) granulated sugar
juice of 1 lemon
1½lb (675g) apricots, halved and pitted
2 egg whites

Put the sugar, ½ pint (300ml) water, and lemon juice into a saucepan and heat gently until the sugar has dissolved. Bring to a boil, add the apricots, and simmer for 15 minutes or until very tender. Cool. Peel and slice a few apricots for decoration, and set aside. Press the remainder through a sieve. Mix with the syrup in a freezerproof container, then follow the Lime Sorbet recipe (above). Decorate with the sliced apricots before serving.

Pear and ginger sorbet

SERVES 6   128 CALS PER SERVING

⅓ cup (90g) granulated sugar
1 tbsp lemon juice
1½lb (675g) pears, peeled and cored
1 piece of crystallized ginger, finely chopped
2 egg whites
pieces of crystallized ginger to decorate

Put the sugar, ½ pint (300ml) water, and lemon juice into a saucepan and heat gently until the sugar dissolves. Bring to a boil, add the pears, and poach gently, basting with the sugar syrup occasionally, for 20–25 minutes until tender. Cool, then purée in a food processor. Add the crystallized ginger and pour into a freezerproof container, then follow the Lime Sorbet recipe (left). Decorate with crystallized ginger before serving.

Raspberry sorbet

SERVES 6   152 CALS PER SERVING

1lb (500g) raspberries
⅔ cup (175g) granulated sugar
juice of 1 orange
3 egg whites
raspberries and mint sprigs to decorate

Purée the raspberries in a food processor, then push through a sieve to remove the seeds. Put the sugar and 1 pint (600ml) water into a saucepan and heat gently until the sugar dissolves. Bring to a boil, then boil for 5 minutes. Pour into a bowl and cool. Stir in the raspberry purée and orange juice. Pour into a freezerproof container, then follow the Lime Sorbet recipe (top left). Decorate with raspberries and mint sprigs before serving.

CRÊPES SUZETTE

SERVES 4   604 CALS PER SERVING

Ingredients

Crêpes

1 cup all-purpose flour

1 large egg

1 tbsp oil, plus extra
   for frying

1¼ cups milk

Orange sauce

juice of 2 oranges

9 tbsp (1 stick + 1 tbsp)
   unsalted butter

¼ cup granulated sugar

3–4 tbsp orange liqueur
   or brandy

Special equipment

7–8in (18–20cm) nonstick
   frying pan

1 Make the crêpes: sift the flour into a bowl. Make a well in the middle. Mix together the egg, 1 tablespoon oil, and the milk and pour into the well. Gradually beat in the flour to make a fairly thin batter.

2 Heat a little oil in the frying pan, then wipe away the excess oil. Add 2–3 tablespoons batter to the pan, tilting it to coat the bottom evenly. Cook for 45–60 seconds, then turn over and cook the other side for about 30 seconds. Slide the crêpe out onto a warmed plate.

3 Repeat to make 7 more crêpes. Stack the crêpes on top of each other as soon as they are cooked (they will not stick together).

4 Make the orange sauce and fold the crêpes (see box, below). Heat to warm through.

MAKING THE SAUCE AND FOLDING THE CRÊPES

Put the orange juice, butter, sugar, and liqueur or brandy into a large frying pan and boil for 5 minutes until reduced. Place 1 crêpe in the pan, coat with sauce, and fold in half, then in half again. Move to one side of the pan. Add another crêpe. Coat with the sauce and fold as before. Repeat with the remaining crêpes.

FRUIT FRITTERS

MAKES 6   361 CALS PER SERVING

Ingredients

2 apples

3 bananas

juice of ½ lemon

sunflower oil for
  deep-frying

⅓ cup granulated sugar

1 tsp ground cinnamon

Batter

1 cup all-purpose flour

1 tbsp confectioner's sugar

1 large egg, separated

⅔ cup mixed milk and water

1 Quarter, core, and peel the apples. Cut the apples and bananas into bite-sized pieces. Toss the pieces in the lemon juice to prevent discoloration.

2 Make the batter: sift the flour and sugar into a bowl and make a well. Add the egg yolk and a little of the milk mixture and whisk together. Whisk in half of the remaining milk mixture, drawing in the flour to form a smooth batter. Add the remaining milk.

3 Whisk the egg white in a separate clean bowl until stiff but not dry. Fold into the batter until evenly mixed.

4 Heat the oil in a deep-fat fryer to 375°F (190°C). Pat the fruit dry. Dip each piece of fruit into the batter, lower into the hot oil, and cook in batches for 3–4 minutes until golden and crisp. Drain on paper towels and keep warm while cooking the remainder.

5 Combine the granulated sugar and cinnamon, sprinkle generously over the fritters, and serve at once.

BAKED APPLES

SERVES 6   235 CALS EACH

Ingredients

6 apples

½ cup light brown sugar

6 tbsp butter, diced

1 Preheat the oven to 375°F (190°C). Wipe the apples and remove the cores using an apple corer. Make a shallow cut through the skin around the equator of each apple.

2 Put the apples into an ovenproof dish and fill their middles with the sugar and butter. Pour 3 tablespoons of water around the apples.

3 Bake for 40–45 minutes until the apples are soft. Serve hot, spooning all the juices from the dish over the apples.

VARIATION

CITRUS baked apples

Add the finely grated zest of 1 orange or 1 lemon to the light brown sugar.

VARIATION

BAKED apples with mincemeat

Use 4oz (125g) mincemeat instead of the sugar and butter.

POACHED PEARS
with blackberry sauce

SERVES 6 375 CALS PER SERVING

Ingredients

1¾ cups granulated sugar

a few strips of lemon zest

6 pears, peeled, but stem left on

For the blackberry sauce

1lb (500g) blackberries

½ cup granulated sugar

1 Put the sugar, 5 cups water, and lemon peel into a saucepan just large enough to take the pears upright in a single layer.

2 Heat gently, stirring until the sugar has dissolved, then boil rapidly for 2 minutes.

3 Place the pears in the hot syrup, cover with a wet sheet of wax paper (this ensures the top of the pears do not dry out), and bring to a boil. Cover with a lid and simmer gently for 30–45 minutes or until the pears are just tender. Set aside to cool.

4 Put the blackberries and sugar into a pan and cook for 5 minutes or until the juices start to run. Push through a sieve into a bowl to get a thickish purée.

5 When the pears are cold, remove from the syrup and pat dry with paper towels.

6 Serve one pear per person or cut each one in half lengthwise through the stem, remove the core, and serve 2 halves. Drizzle with the sauce.

LEMON CHEESECAKE
on a ginger crust

SERVES 8   493 CALS PER SERVING

Ingredients

1 cup crushed gingersnaps

3 tbsp butter, melted

2 x 9oz (250g) tubs full-fat
  mascarpone

1 x 11½oz (325g) jar
  lemon curd

juice of 1 small lemon

fresh raspberries and
  blueberries, to decorate

confectioner's sugar, to dust

Special equipment

8in (20cm) round loose-
  bottomed cake pan,
  greased, and bottom lined
  with parchment paper

1 Mix the gingersnaps with the butter in a bowl, then press into the bottom of the pan (but not up the sides).

2 Put the mascarpone, lemon curd, and lemon juice in a bowl and beat with a spatula until smooth.

3 Spoon onto the cookie crust and level the top. Chill in the fridge for at least 4 hours and up to 24 hours to firm up.

4 To serve, remove the cheesecake from the pan, peel off the parchment paper, and arrange on a platter. Decorate with the fruit and dust with confectioner's sugar.

Great for a crowd

You can make up to three cheesecakes in one batch (but be careful not to overbeat the mixture at step 2). If you're making more cheesecakes than that, prepare them in separate batches.

BAKED APPLE
dumplings

SERVES 4   781 CALS PER SERVING

Ingredients

Dumpling dough

3 cups all-purpose flour

6 tbsp chilled butter, cut
  into cubes, plus
  extra for greasing

3oz (90g) chilled
  vegetable shortening,
  cut into cubes

For the apples

4 tart apples, peeled
  and cored

¼ cup brown sugar

½ tsp ground cinnamon

milk for glazing

1 Preheat the oven to 400°F (200°C). Make the dough: put the flour into a large bowl. Add the butter and vegetable shortening and rub in with your fingertips until the mixture resembles fine bread crumbs. Mix in enough cold water (about 3–4 tablespoons) to make a soft, pliable dough. Wrap the dough in plastic wrap and chill for about 30 minutes.

2 Divide the dough into 4 pieces. Roll out each piece on a lightly floured surface and cut into a 7in (18cm) round. Reserve the trimmings. Put an apple in the center of each round and make 4 dumplings (see box, below).

3 Cut leaf shapes from the dough trimmings and use to decorate the tops of the dumplings, attaching them with a little water. Make a hole in the top of each dumpling and lightly brush all over with milk.

4 Bake for 35–40 minutes until the dough is golden and the apples are tender. Serve hot.

MAKING THE APPLE DUMPLINGS

Fill the apples with the brown sugar and cinnamon. Draw up a dough round to enclose each apple, sealing the seams with a little water. Place, with the seams underneath, on a baking sheet.

RUM AND RAISIN
ice cream

SERVES 10–12 239–286 CALS EACH

Ingredients

1½ cups raisins

5 tbsp dark rum

4 large eggs, separated

½ cup granulated sugar

1¼ cups heavy cream

Special equipment

2-quart (2-liter) freezerproof
   container

1 Put the raisins into a bowl and add the rum. Let soak—
ideally overnight.

2 Put the egg yolks into a small bowl and whisk with a fork
until blended.

3 Whisk the egg whites with a handheld electric mixer until they look
like clouds. Whisking on maximum speed, add the sugar a teaspoon
at a time until the mixture is stiff and glossy.

4 Whip the cream until soft peaks form, then fold into the egg white
mixture until smooth. Stir in the egg yolks and soaked raisins. If
there is any rum left in the bowl, add this, too.

5 Transfer to the freezerproof container
and freeze for a minimum of 24 hours.

6 Remove from the freezer 10 minutes
before serving to make
scooping easier.

Rum and raisin ice cream

This unique and beautiful
flavor pairing originated in
Italy—the home of ice cream.
The great thing about this
recipe is that you don't need
an ice cream maker.

Index